BECOMING GOD'S
21ST CENTURY AMBASSADOR

A Young Girl's Jaw-Dropping Testimony

By Dr. Nicku Kyungu Mordi

BECOMING GOD'S 21ST CENTURY AMBASSADOR

A Young Girl's Jaw-Dropping Testimony

Then I heard the voice of the Lord saying,
"Whom shall I send? And who will go for us?"
And I said, "Here am I. Send me!" ⁹ He said,
"Go and tell 'How Much I Love Them!'
Isaiah 6:8-9a

Dr. Nicku Kyungu Mordi

Becoming God's 21st Century Ambassador

ISBN: 978-0-9995855-7-3

Published by Lams Publishing , United Kingdom
publish@lamsenterprise.com

Cover Design by Lisa Sims
Printed in the United States of America

PREFACE

You will agree that you are created to do more than what you are doing now! Often, my heart is disturbed when I see the most powerful institution on earth operating beneath her potential. The purpose of this book is to stimulate the Church to the phenomenal vitality power for missions in contemporary Christianity, and to remind the Church of the marvelous privilege as well as a great responsibility God has given her to disciple the nations. A new day of challenge and opportunity has arrived for individuals to heed God's call to see the harvest and help churches prepare their people for missions. This book will also stimulate individual change-from casual perception of the Word of God to a desire to have an experiential phenomenal dimension of living in the Kingdom lifestyle.

It is also designed to give a personal mission account in order to encourage others to further the cause of the Great

Commission, a cause that has been my lifelong passion and focus. I thank God who has given us everything in Christ. As a young girl, I told Jesus I would do anything as an outlet for love and gratitude, knowing there is nothing I can repay Him. He has done so much for us. Many times, I stay silently before His presence with unspeakable awe and joy for choosing me as His ambassador to "GO" and evangelize nations.

Today's mission field is not in the far country but right in your neighborhood. It is not an expansion of Christianity among people who have not heard about Christ alone, but it includes going to places where people are Christians but they are not taught proper doctrine or growing in the Christian Faith. Reading this book will help those who desire to use their faith to do great things for God starting where they are and using what they have. Also, I pray that some leaders will hear Jesus tell them, "Take off the grave clothes on God's people and let them GO to witness!" This is the message He told those who bound Lazarus!

I thank God for the many people in my life who have allowed me to live my God given purpose. Thanks to all the I GO Ministries Team leaders and supporters. A special grateful expression of indebtedness must be made to my biological family, especially my Sister Eneah Joel Milanes who believes in my calling and has been my constant supporter. I praise God for all the great friends I met in different parts of the world. You are all appreciated.

Finally, to my God given husband George N. Mordi and our two girls, you are the best crown of my life. Often you have said, "wife or mom, don't be an illusion; things don't work that way in really world!" My answer has often been, "My faith world is different- that is why you don't see it" Thank you for understanding the God given assignment for me.

DEDICATION

This book is dedicated to my three grandchildren:
D.J., Jalynn and Ezra. May God's purpose be fulfilled in
your lives as you live to obey His Word
(*Joshua 1:7-8; I Timothy 4:12*).
I love you very much.

CONTENTS

INTRODUCTION

Nikita Khrushchev was the Russian President of the Communist Party of the Soviet Union, popularly known as the USSR (Union of Soviet Socialist Republics) which existed from 1922-1991. Their motto was "Workers of the World United" and their main religion was "atheism". Karl Marx published a Communist Manifesto addressing the history of class struggles in society. The working class was going to bring the end of class society – though it had little impact, its ideas reverberated into the 20th century. By 1950, nearly half of the world's population was under Marxist government.

Marx was also editor of Rheinische Zaitung, a liberal democratic Newspaper in Cologne, Germany, however by 1843, the newspaper was shut down. Marx then moved to Paris to co-edit a new political review nicknamed **"Marx-Zeitung"** which adopted a more extreme form of socialism that called for a revolution of working-class people to tear down the capitalist world. Why am I writing this as an introductory of this book?

What has the dismantled USSR got to do with you in the 21st century? I am glad you asked!

Opening with such an introduction has to do with giving the reader another dimension to understand more of how God uses unconventional ways when we are available to serve in any capacity. As we obey to do His will by going "into all the world," God has supernatural ways to use any method that is unconceivable to a human mind. As a young girl in 1977, God sent me to be a missionary/evangelist in Sweden and the entire Northern Europe. In 1978, I was going to preach in the communist USSR. It was against the law to evangelize or to have any religious materials. Nevertheless, I took Bibles in my luggage and one Bible in my hand luggage to read as I travelled. However, I purposely disguised it with a red cover so it would not be noticed as a Bible.

I flew from Helsinki, Finland to St Petersburg, USSR. As I was riding a train to Moscow, the plain-clothed KGBs as well as other uniformed police went around the train cabins to check passports and other travelling documents. Foreigners were especially searched. They looked carefully into all their belongings. Those who were found with anything that was prohibited were not allowed in the USSR. They were yelled at and taken off the compartment to a special interrogating place. I saw a beautiful girl being put in handcuffs. As I looked at what was taking place, my antenna connected with the frequency of Jehovah and I found myself reminding Him that it was the perfect time *"to cover me with His feathers, and under His wings I should find refuge" (Psalms 91:4a)*. I told Him that those Russian officials should not see anything because it was His responsibility to blind them. Then I boldly opened my Bible pretending I was reading while I continued to commune with HIM.

When the inspectors came into our compartment, they were serious and took my Bible out of my hand, flipped the pages and they began to have a smile on their faces and said to me, "good Marx-Zeitung Book!!" Those words came from each person who held the Bible, in fact one even showed his comrade and they were glad to see the "Marx-Zeitung book" As they flipped the pages to see if I was hiding anything, I kept on thanking God in my mind and spirit, yet I was shocked about what was happening! It was a supernatural miracle! God was protecting His "missionary girl" from the oppressive regime. Instead of being caught and thrown in prison by entering with Bibles in a communist nation, God blinded their eyes to see their communist manifesto! Above all, they did not even search my suitcase nor did they look at my passport. God is faithful to protect His own. The Bible says:

"For the eyes of the LORD range throughout the earth to strengthen those whose hearts are fully committed to him." (2 Chronicles 16:9a)

"He will cover you with his feathers, and under his wings you will find refuge his faithfulness will be your shield and rampart." (Psalms 91:4)

CHAPTER ONE
DISMANTLING THE COMMUNITY

When you are born, you enroll in the school of life of which we are all students. When we grow up, one has to be wise as to which life's classes to enroll in and master because every stage, every incident, every feeling and every season has a different syllabus. One has to know that learning only stops when death gives you your final examination and heaven hands you your diploma! However, some of God's children do not live to their potential because they hand over the God-image-bearing nature to other idols. Today's idols are camouflaged in concepts and social ideas that have no absolute. They dedicate their time and strength, and even allow unworthy things to determine their identity, self-worth or esteem.

The idols that we give power to, whether physical or not, rob us of our true nature and identity. Even what consumes our thoughts, if it is not in line with the Word of God, becomes a hindrance to what our lives ought to be. Since God called me at the age of six years and separated me, I try hard to live and simply believe what the word says, such as "the earth is the Lord's!" In my mind I reason very simply, "if it is the Lord's, then I have the responsibility to make it better," Psalms 33:5 says, "*The LORD loves righteousness and justice; the earth is full of his unfailing love*". Proverb 21:3 also says "*To do what is right and just is more acceptable to the LORD than sacrifice. These show me that I must be the one to demonstrate His justice and unfailing love.*" Also Psalms 23:6 is one of my favorites. Listen to what it says: "*Surely your goodness and love will follow me all the days of my life, and I will dwell in the house of the LORD FOREVER.*" Since the earth is the Lords, there are no limitations to where He might send His children. Above all, anywhere you are, remember He promises that His goodness and love will follow you. That should make any child of God smile and be willing to obey Him.

However, before answering the call to "GO" to a world unknown to me, I was a well to do young lady zealous for God and had a good job working in Nairobi, Kenya. However, in 1973 our employer, the East Africa Railways and Harbors was dissolving- the agreement of the East African Community (Kenya, Tanzania and Uganda) was in dispute. Each country had to recall her citizens from Kenya. When my older sister, Eneah Joel (fondly called Enjo) heard this nationalization, she started planning for my return to Tanzania and told me to start applying for a job in Dar es Salaam. I had never known how to apply for a job but I was quick to talk to God about it. After a day or so my friend told me about a West Africa Cocoa company from Ghana looking for secretaries in Dar es Salaam. She told me she had already done the paperwork for both of us and we had to wait. After a week I was selected to go for the interview instead of my friend who told me about it. She was nice and did not mind me going. I flew to Dar es Salaam for an interview.

The information told us the interview was being held at the New Africa Hotel facing the Indian Ocean in the city center of Dar es Salaam, Tanzania. I was optimistic about getting the job and I started visualizing my departure to move to Accra, Ghana in West Africa to work in the Cocoa Company. When I arrived, the hotel receptionist directed me to take the elevator to the fifth floor and he gave me the suite number where the interview was being held. It was a quiet morning. I reached the room and knocked with confidence. When the door opened, I saw only one man wearing a hotel robe! It was strange, but I thought other people are in the next room. I also assumed that he was not involved in the interview process since he was not properly dressed.

As I entered, I started to introduce myself while he was closing the door. He interrupted and said my name, "Nicku, I am glad you are here. I know you will enjoy working in Ghana," as he pulled a chair for me to sit. At that moment, my spirit, soul and body shouted within me "DANGER" because I did not hear any sound from the other room. While still on my feet I asked, "Sir, where are the other interviewers? I was told three or four people will be conducting the interview." He hesitated a bit and then said, "we will meet them later after I have had time to know you! Meanwhile he was trying to reach for my hand to pull me closer to him. I lifted my handbag, pushed him aside, reached for the door and ran out the room to the elevator.

Since I was young, I had surrendered my life to Christ. I was not just a religious girl, but I was a child of God who purposed to please my Father. As I grew up, I loved to read His Word and to tell others about the joy of living in righteousness. I could not let anything come between my Lord and me. In that moment, I remembered what I had read which said, 'FREE/RUN" from sexual immorality! That was the intention of the man in the room. In such a situation, it was not the time to start to evangelize or to preach to him but to obey what the Word says:

> "*Flee from sexual immorality. All other sins a person commits are outside the body, but whoever sins sexually, sins against their own body. 19 Do you not know that your bodies are temples of the Holy Spirit, who is in you, whom you have received from God? You are not your own; 20 you were bought at a price. Therefore, honor God with your bodies.*" (I Corinthians 6:18-20)

Because God is our Father, He has given us a will! In my case I chose to obey God with everything, including my body! As I ran towards the elevator, I was furious, talking to myself, "who does he think I am? I entered the elevator without paying attention, not knowing I was still talking aloud. One of the three men in the elevator asked, "what is the matter young lady- you seem so angry?" Without knowing who they were, and because I did not expect anyone to have heard, I vividly remember saying, "this foolish man wanted to kiss me. I came to the hotel for a job interview but he said he has to know me first. Besides, he was wearing a hotel robe. What kind of interview is that?" One guy answered me and said, "calm down lady, that is how this culture is -if you want something you give something!" I turned to him even more upset and said, "Sir, if that is your culture, I am not part of it. You can keep your job and your money." Another man said, "you speak good English. I am from USAID and we are looking for workers in different departments. Come we will interview you." I believe I had a mean look as I said, "No thanks, I do not need any interview in Dar. I am flying back to Nairobi." The elevator reached the ground floor and I rushed out quickly, angrier, and without saying a word to the men in the elevator. I was still sad and stupid!

After a while, I felt sorry for the nice men in the elevator because I vented on them. At the same time, I was angry at myself because I did not know how I could have walked into such a trap! While working at the Railways Headquarters, I had heard how some girls got positions because they slept with their bosses or someone. I could not comprehend this. Before I went for the interview, it slightly crossed my mind as to why the interview was being held in a Hotel!! But the answer came quickly and was clear, "the Ghanaian Cocoa Company had no representatives. They came to establish their regional office in Tanzania and had to start using the hotel." Secondly, I like to give people the benefit of a doubt. I trust people, and that also had put me in trouble if I refuse to compromise my faith and moral standards.

Nevertheless, God has been faithful to protect me from different traps of the enemy because He knows my heart, my inner attitude towards what I do and my desire to live for Him. Above all, God has shown all of His children His desire of how much He cares for each one of them.

"No temptation has overtaken you except what is common to mankind. And God is faithful; he will not let you be tempted[b] beyond what you can bear. But when you are tempted,[c] he will also provide a way out so that you can endure it."(I Corinthians 10:13)

When you surrender your life to Him, and you purpose to allow Christ to live in you in spirit and truth, and you practice holiness by obeying the Word, be assured there will be different kinds of challenges, temptations and situations that you will face. But I can assure you, you can overcome and be victorious because of Christ in you! You have to know that the Jesus you talk about, or sing about or pray to is the same Jesus who gives you power to overcome any temptation or challenge. It is no longer you that fight the battles, but Christ in you.

In the evening, I left Dar es Salaam without any interview. When I reached home, I told my sister about the scenario and then I continued, "I somehow understood a bit why girls or women find themselves doing what they did not expect. Life is hard without Jesus." Indeed, without Christ and without knowing the power invested in us through the accomplished work on the cross, it is hard to live a victorious life in this corrupt world, especially if you are looking to improve your life and you have to deal with "unjust people or corrupt bosses".

My sister encouraged me to apply at the USAID since they were looking for workers. But I was not interested. After a few weeks, my sister came laughing and said, "Nicku I met one of my friends who works in the USAID, he told me about what they discussed in their staff meeting!! They were talking about a young lady they met in the elevator who had high moral values but was not from Dar. They really wanted to find out who she was, so they asked some of us to be on the lookout if we hear about the "interview gone bad"! When I heard what my sister was saying, I started paying close attention as she continued, "I knew he was referring to you but I did not say anything. You left an impression in the elevator my little sister and now they want to employ you." I stopped paying attention because I was not interested in being employed by them. My sister always wanted the best for us, especially me. She went behind my back to tell the USAID man that the girl they met in the elevator was her little sister. He was surprised and promised her that I would be hired immediately if I went back to Dar es Salaam. Was that a coincidence or was God's hand in it?

One evening my sister said, "Nicku, in two weeks' time, you are moving back to Tanzania because all the Railway employees have to go to their nations." I could not say anything except to agree with her. When I went back to the East Africa Railways Headquarters to pick up my things, many of the girls had secured employment with the Harbors Headquarters in Dar. I was left out because I had confidently told them that when the East African Community folded, I was going to work with the Cocoa Company in Ghana, West Africa. I had nothing to worry about looking for a job anywhere. So, when I returned from Tanzania without a job, they all laughed at me. I recall one girl saying to me, "Nicku we are also Christians. You do not have to live in the artificial world of faith. Look at yourself now-you have no job because you refused a simple kiss!" Other girls giggled and gave me a despising look. When she was talking, my heart wanted to explode! My mouth wanted to

---

talk back, but I controlled myself. I did not say a word because I knew what Psalms 37:8 and Colossians 3:8-10 says:

"Refrain from anger and turn from wrath; do not fret— it leads only to evil." (Psalms 37:8)

"But now you must also rid yourselves of all such things as these: anger, rage, malice, slander, and filthy language from your lips. ⁹ Do not lie to each other, since you have taken off your old self with its practices ¹⁰ and have put on the new self, which is being renewed in knowledge in the image of its Creator." (Colossians 3:8-10)

Though it was my last week at work and I did not know if I would get a job, I did not panic because I knew God is my Father and His goodness and mercy will follow me anywhere, as the Word of God says. The more the other girls shared their plans, I put my trust in God. Some of them seemed to have gotten good jobs while others decided to remain in Nairobi rather than go back. I kept telling them "I am not my own, so I will not panic because my Father is in control"

CHAPTER TWO
LIFE IS GOOD IN TANZANIA

Don't worry ....[30] *If that is how God clothes the grass of the field, which is here today and tomorrow is thrown into the fire, will he not much more clothe you—you of little faith?* [31] *So do not worry, saying, 'What shall we eat?' or 'What shall we drink?' or 'What shall we wear?'* [32] *For the pagans run after all these things, and your heavenly Father knows that you need them.* [33] *But seek first his kingdom and his righteousness, and all these things will be given to you as well.* [34] *Therefore do not worry about tomorrow, for tomorrow will worry about itself. Each day has enough trouble of its own.* (Matthew 6:30-34)

A few days after our office closed, I received information to report for work at the USAID in Dar es Salaam. I was shocked because I did not apply, yet at the same time I was excited, giving God the praise. Immediately, I left Nairobi and moved to Dar es Salaam. On my first day I went directly to the American Embassy to report for duty and I started working as a secretary to the Commercial Attaché. After a week or so, two officers who seemed to be debating something entered our office and one said, "young lady, what are you doing here? We have been expecting you at the USAID and now you are working in our Embassy?" I looked puzzled because I did not know what he was talking about and said, "Sir I thought this is where I am to work. Should I have gone somewhere else?" I was genuinely not sure what he was talking about. Seeing the shocked on my face, the Embassy Administrative Officer smiled and said to me, "Nicku, don't listen to him, you are working here now," Then he told the other officer, "sorry my friend, return to your office and go look for another one because Nicku will stay here." Both walked out of the office without saying a word.

After they left, I was still puzzled by what they were talking about! I asked Mr. Suleman, my immediate supervisor who shared his office with me, why the other gentleman said, "Why was I there?" Mr. Suleman laughed and started to educate me how the USAID was different from the US Embassy!!! I am sorry to admit I was very naive in so many things! I still have a long way to learn! In 1973 I was very young and naïve. I had no idea they were two different entities. It also continued to puzzle me, "how could they give me a job and an office without any interview?" I wondered!! After a few minutes of trying to figure it out, I felt the Spirit whisper to me, "It is your Father who is working on your behalf – the entire earth is His and everything in it, including this Embassy, belongs to your Father!" Such thoughts filled my mind and I did not worry about what I could not understand because I knew my Father was in control!

I focused on what I knew best, praising Him while thinking of the scenario that took place and rewinding my memory to the previous month when I rushed out of the hotel room. How could I meet someone in the elevator who worked with the USAID? What I thought was venting to the innocent people in the elevator, God turned into a job interview! God's ways cannot be understood!! How could someone relate to my older sister what was discussed in the USAID Office about my behavior and much more? Regardless of what you might think, I give God the glory for looking out for me. He gave me the best prestigious job to work with the Embassy of the United States of America, the most powerful nation on earth. The only thing I could do was to repeat what the Word says in 2 Chronicles 16:9 :

> "Now to the King eternal, immortal, invisible, the only God, be honor and glory for ever and ever. Amen."

As well as knowing God is God, "In the LORD's hand the king's heart is a stream of water that he channels toward all who please him." (Proverbs 21:1)

It was very easy to compromise or backslide working in the embassy. We also had strict rules to follow .Talking about God was out of the question but we were encouraged to be friendly, professional and dress well. Their rules gave me zeal and wisdom on how to demonstrate my faith in whatever I did. First, people misunderstood me and thought I was given a job because I had a relationship with some boss at the Embassy. All kinds of human thinking went on because they could not believe how I got the job. It is amazing how people want to pull you into their-mediocre behavior and life experience and want you to be just like them- "ordinary." Also, I understood that people do not really depend on God's word for their daily living – they only use the Word in church or among religious activities. That is why it was hard for them to understand my uniqueness of living the Word. It is true that many people had applied and were interviewed for several weeks, yet I got the job because God ordered my steps.

It is sad to think that no one believed it when I said I lived differently because I depended on someone bigger than anyone in their midst! I often told them, "Jesus is my boss and He was the one who opened the Embassy doors. He will do the same for you if you put Him first." When they heard me talk like that, they thought I was crazy. But as the years rolled by, they observed that I remained consistent, and overcame every obstacle and every entrapment. The Bible says, *"by their fruits, you shall know them that they are His followers,"* (Matthew 7:16-20). I became a very respected young lady. My steadfastness spread among diplomats, expatriates, civil servants and government offices across the city.

Admirers and destroyers were coming from different directions, and some of them received Jesus as their Lord. Others thought I was wasting my youth by not being flexible or discerning the times! Regardless of what they said, my choice was to be Light and Salt anywhere I was even in the who is who in society! Some diplomats from the African Embassies tried all the tricks to make me compromise! I was not intimidated. I made them friends because I wanted everyone to fall in love with the personal Jesus, not a religious figure who has no power. I knew and I was always mindful that God put me there among diplomats to be His Ambassador.

Working in the commercial section of the US Embassy, connected me with many visitors who came to promote American businesses to be introduced in Tanzania. We used to have different parties and receptions. Often, American women from the embassy and some visitors came to my house to get some of my African attire to wear. I recall when Henry Kissinger came, four visitors requested to wear my clothes. It was great to see them enjoy my African outfits at the Kilimanjaro Hotel Reception. I was having so much fun at work, and in my Ilala Assemblies of God Church, as well as with other churches around the city. Living for God and obeying His Word is what I desire everyone to experience- it is much easier than being religious. In those days I was very popular and loved to dress well for His glory. My family spoiled me, especially my elder sister Enjo who used to buy me all kinds of classy, expensive and unique outfits so that I could shine for Jesus.

Being God's witness or His missionary girl as we will read later, does not mean you have to be dull or travel to a far country. Being a witness of Christ should be a lifestyle, and we must be the happiest people on earth. My life attracted people of all walks of life. My home was like a meeting place. The three bedroom house with a huge dining area entertained many dignitaries: American missionaries and visitors; Religious leaders; Bishops, Assemblies of God Superintendents and other Church leaders; International Speakers like Morris Cerullo of California, USA; Holmes Williams of Barbados, West Indies and Senator Mac Nwulu of Aba, Nigeria. Friends and strangers came to my house for dinner, refreshments and parties on different occasions.

I never dreamed I could leave my country or my great job. I was very comfortable being involved in the things I loved: evangelizing, and early prayer meetings at St. Columbus Anglican church where I met a missionary/pastor who invited me to preach in Glasgow, UK in 1976. I also used to hold open air meetings under the Assemblies of God Churches and we saw many people accept Jesus Christ. My mission field started in my own country with my own people. I had my own car to run around picking up people for different spiritual meetings. Those days, you could hardly see young girls driving or owning cars! God's favor and His grace enabled me to live above the norm because I practiced His scripture that says:

His divine power has given us everything we need for a
godly life through our knowledge of him who called
us by his own glory and goodness.(2 Peter 1:3)

Life was very good in Tanzania; I had no plans to leave until God interrupted my life to become *His missionary girl.* He came and told me like He told Abraham in Genesis 12:1 *"Go from your country, your people and your father's household to the land I will show you."* Hearing those words hit me like a brick! I did not know where God wanted me to go, nor did I want to start explaining to my boss at the Embassy why I was leaving after being there for only three years! Also, for an African girl to say you are led by the Holy Spirit to do anything, was not embedded in our Christian teachings. It seemed as if the Holy Spirit was absent in our daily living. After questioning and doubting if I heard right, I was certain it was Him speaking! God once again wanted me to get out of my comfort zone and out of my homeland and 'GO"! This is what Matthew 28:18-20 says:

Then Jesus came to them and said, "All authority in
heaven and on earth has been given to me. ¹⁹ Therefore
go and make disciples of all nations, baptizing them in
the name of the Father and of the Son and of the Holy

Spirit, [20] and teaching them to obey everything I have commanded you. And surely, I am with you always, to the very end of the age."

Knowing God had spoken and that He promised to be with me, I started preparing myself psychologically, and emotionally, and sharing with my family. Before I told my boss, I had to seek wisdom from above so that it would not upset them. Politely I said, "Sir, I might leave the Embassy anytime that God tells me the date to go!" No one at the Embassy could understand, some thought I was joking around. I recall one officer said I could not be called to missions because I was a Tanzanian. Some did not want to see me leave, especially because working with the Embassy is supposed to be a prestigious position. They gave me all kinds of reasons but I paid them no attention. I was God's Girl who totally believed in what the Word of God says in Matthew 6:33 _"But seek first his kingdom and his righteousness, and all these things will be given to you as well."_ Sometime around May, the Holy Spirit gave me confirmation to leave Tanzania in July 1977 and go to Sweden in Scandinavia.

The statement that was spoken by the American officer in the embassy "I could not be sent anywhere because I was a

Tanzanian" kept flashing in my mind, especially in regards to going to Sweden!!! That sure did not make sense. I started questioning God like Moses did in Exodus 33:12-17. Although the assignment was different, for a young 26-year-old African girl, the responsibility of going to Sweden without any contact or sponsor was frightening...

"Moses said to the LORD, "You have been telling me, 'Lead these people,' but you have not let me know whom you will send with me. You have said, 'I know you by name and you have found favor with me.' 13 If you are pleased with me, teach me your ways so I may know you and continue to find favor with you. Remember that this nation is your people." 14 The LORD replied, "My Presence will go with you, and I will give you rest." .... 16 How will anyone know that you are pleased with me and .... What else will distinguish me and your people from all the other people on the face of the earth?"17 And the LORD said to Moses, "I will do the very thing you have asked, because I am pleased with you and I know you by name." (Exodus 33:12-17)

Those words became revelatory to me and gave me strength not to fear or to take seriously anything other people spoke to discourage me. "God's favor was upon me and He was pleased by my child-like faith of always saying "obeying God is better than doing any kind of activity or service for Him!" (1 Samuel 15:22). Above all, "He knew me by name" became my Rhema Word. Nevertheless, He gave me a date to leave to go to a mission field in Sweden, Northern Europe without giving me any other clue of how to start!

Abraham was told to go to a "place God was showing him" and there he would be a blessing to others. Obeying God always has abundant blessings. However, His blessings to us are not measured by who we are or what we have done but who God is – He is our Father. The blessings can be experienced in different ways – salvation, family, friends, provision, protection, good health and many more. Christians have the "now blessings" and the "future blessings" of eternal life. Therefore, with any blessing that comes to any Christian, God exhorts us to be a blessing to others. He wants us to be a living channel of God's blessings – physical and spiritual. God never created us to be reservoirs. Abraham was promised that he would be a blessing when he left his home and his family, "You shall be a blessing to others." (Genesis 12:2)

Indeed, Abraham obeyed God, took his family and they started going to "nowhere". I am sure everyone thought he was crazy! Can you imagine telling your wife and children- next week we are leaving! Then when they ask you, "where are we going Daddy?"- you look at them in the face and say, "I don't know, just get ready we are leaving!" I cannot imagine for you, but I will try to tell what the wife told the kids, "don't worry children, Dad is joking. How can we leave to go nowhere?!!" Fortunately, when God was calling me to missions, I was not married nor did I have any children, but it was very hard to leave all the great things I had and what I was doing for the community, family and church.

As I was struggling, God said, "your separation was pivotal to helping many other people love me and nations being blessed." I could not comprehend what God was telling me but I decided to blindly obey Him, knowing Jesus made Himself of no reputation for my sake. This is a lesson for the Christians who struggle to obey God, or those who want to know all the details before they obey God. I am writing my own testimony to help you learn and know what to do in order to fulfill the Great Commission by doing simple and ordinary things. By faith, and with peace in my heart, in July 1977 I left Tanzania with all my possessions behind and reached a country I never knew. By faith I arrived in Sweden as a missionary/evangelist.

CHAPTER THREE
NO WAY! AN AFRICAN GIRL?
ON A MISSION?

It was amazing how no one could believe I was leaving my country and all its comforts in order to obey God. Many refused to believe what I was saying except to rely on their own human opinions. I believe one of the reasons people don't understand to "walk in the spirit", is because the missionary churches that we grew up in came from the background that neglected the role of the Holy Spirit in the post Reformation era. There was also an unconscious factor that the Great Commission was not to be accomplished by ordinary people except clergies in the Five-Fold Ministries and foreign missionaries. Although I was an Elder in the Assemblies of God Church, that was also a miracle because back then women were not encouraged to be in ministry or ordained for ministry. Also, I had missionary friends from the USA, they discouraged me, out of concern, not to leave. Throughout the preparation, I was hearing discouraging words how it was not proper for me to leave my country and "GO" as His witness. They felt it did not make sense. I wondered if all those Christians understood what Acts 1:8 says,

> "But you will receive power when the Holy Spirit comes on you; and you will be my witnesses in Jerusalem, and in all Judea and Samaria, and to the ends of the earth."

It seemed no one thought I was qualified to be His witness to the "ends of the earth." Why couldn't I be like other Christian girls who serve God faithfully without being too extreme? Yes, many thought I was taking the Word of God to the extreme! Nevertheless, I had my earthly Dad, Mzee Joel Kyungu Mwakasege, who encouraged me to obey God even if it did not make sense! He added, "obeying God does not mean you will understand Him - you have to walk by faith" He reminded me how God had been with me as I travelled across East Africa (Kenya, Uganda & Tanzania) to preach and witness. My father said, "He will be with you even if He sends you to Europe. He is the same God."

Leaving my good job and all I had, in obedience to God, was not easily understood by many people. It had never happened before in our country, even across Africa. In reality, even I did not understand what I was doing, especially when people I knew and depended upon kept questioning how I knew it was God sending me overseas! The only confidence I had, and I kept on telling them was, "the Holy Spirit has spoken audibly to me." They did not get it and I could not say anything that made sense to them!

During that lonely time, is when I fell in love with the old song written by a Southern Gospel Evangelist and songwriter Ira F. Stanphil who died in 1993 in Overland Park, Kansas after writing over 500 Gospel songs and hymns. Thank God for using people in different nations to spread His universal love and hope. This song gave me courage because I really did not know what I was getting into: deciding to leave all behind without any other plan except to obey God who did not give me any details of the journey, was indeed crazy in modern day terminology. You have to plan before you travel anywhere! Walking by faith requires different frequencies. Maybe you are going through challenging times. Maybe what you expected to be the outcome of your plans have turned out to be a disappointment. Take time and sing this song with me. You will feel His presence as you remind yourself that life is filled with many unknown things.

"I don't know about tomorrow;

I just live for day to day

I don't borrow from the sunshine;

For its skies may turn to gray

I don't worry over the future;

For I know what Jesus said

And today I'll walk beside Him;

For He knows what lies ahead

Many things about tomorrow,

I don't seem to understand

But I know who holds tomorrow,

And I know who holds my hand!"

(Ira F. Stanphil)

Indeed, life is filled with uncertainty and inconsistencies, but we can depend on the Holy Spirit who was given for our benefit. Luke 12:12 says, *"for the Holy Spirit will teach you at that time what you should say."* I had to depend on Him who never changes nor forsakes us. Although the church preaches about the Holy Spirit, there is little understanding for the people in the pews, or for individuals to connect the

---

Holy Spirit with the assignment of fulfilling the Great Commission. In the lives of many Christians there is a demise of the experiential dimension of the Christian faith. In this context, when I shared about my calling, there should have been no question or suspicion of being sent 'by God' to be a missionary. This should be common to all who believe in the Lordship of Christ and what He commanded us to do.

When Christ dwells within a believer by the Spirit and the believer gets filled with the power of the Holy Spirit , the primary motivating factor to that believer is to be a witness, and not to only speak in tongues. Going into missions (wherever that might be) to spread the Good News, is the function of the Holy Spirit to lead you. It should not have seemed to be a unique phenomenon for an African girl to be sent overseas. God can call anyone from anywhere because the harvest is plenteous! However, you can give them the benefit of the doubt because in the 1970s, it was never heard of an African leaving their country for a sole purpose of being a "missionary" in Europe. To complicate the scenarios, I was not being sent by any church or organization, and that is why no one could understand. People believed and thought only

Europeans or Americans were the ones to be "missionaries" and not young African girls!

I thank God that western missionaries did great things in Africa. May God reward their efforts and sacrifices. However, some of them failed to respond positively and biblically to the African needs. Biblical revelation provides ample solutions to deal with such mindsets. Also, some of the positions they took, of God-against-culture, created an inferiority complex in the African mind. Thus, many Africans thought it must be a white people's organization that was sending me to Sweden! I am sure you have experienced Christians who sincerely believe God and are filled with the Holy Spirit, but yet they are the ones who oppose spiritual things more than others. The reason is because they are not yet transformed by the power of God. Their knowledge of God through His Word is entirely conceptual rather than experiential.

At the same time, the Church has forgotten that she is an organ of the Spirit's expression for missions to encourage members to "GO". This negative attitude toward the Holy Spirit has daily eroded the expectancy of His leading and has contributed to the inability of many Christians to enter into their full potential of living in the present Kingdom of God. Even if the church teaches or encourages her members to be involved in missions, it has to be a person's desire and hunger to get involved. No one can force anyone to be or do what Christ commanded us to do. Matthew 5:6 says, *"Blessed are those who hunger and thirst for righteousness, for they will be filled."* I have chosen to hunger for His intimate relationship and to tune my spiritual ears to anticipate hearing God when He speaks-not only to hear but also to obey Him even if I do not understand, which is more than I can count!

This kind of faith comes when you get the revelation of who God is in the context of your own life. Have a fundamental belief that God is present today in your Christian experience, and that the ministry of the Holy Spirit is available to guide you. With such revelation and conviction, you will live in expectancy of His communication and intervention in your daily life. This is the Kingdom lifestyle God wants His children to experience. This is what I have chosen and I try to live it, and totally depend on what the Holy Spirit says in John 14: 16, 26.

"And I will ask the Father, and he will give you another advocate to help you and be with you forever.......But the

Advocate, the Holy Spirit, whom the Father will send in my name, will teach you all things and will remind you of everything I have said."

Jesus left us with powerful promises that can help us to "go into all nations/professions/vocations/and places of power" because of the guidance and leading of the Holy Spirit. Furthermore, in John 16:13-15, Jesus said:

"But when he, the Spirit of truth, comes, he will guide you into all the truth. He will not speak on his own; he will speak only what he hears, and he will tell you what is yet to come. [14] He will glorify me because it is from me that he will receive what he will make known to you.
[15] All that belongs to the Father is mine. That is why I said the Spirit will receive from me what he will make known to you."

In the 1970s there were many misconceptions about the Holy Spirit. Many believed and taught that His miracles ceased during the disciples' days. There were those who believed in the power of the Holy Spirit, but they limited Him to speaking in tongues, casting out evil spirits and performing miracles, but not with connecting the Holy Spirit to the Great Commission. God's Spirit is given to equip believers to be bold witnesses. For example, Peter, the disciple gave the divine revelation to who Jesus was. He said to Jesus" *You are the Christ, the Son of the Living God"* (Matt. 16:16). However, during the passion of Christ, Peter was coward and timid before a slave girl (Matt.26:28, 69-72) The reason Peter denied Jesus is because he was limited, even though He was a follower of Jesus. It is not enough to belong to the best church or to be part of any church leadership, nor is it enough to have theological accreditations or be called to preach – without the personal experience of the baptism of the Holy Spirit you will be limited and you will be easily swayed by all kinds of teachings, opinions and lifestyle.

Imagine! I left my country without having any specific location where to go except the name "Sweden!" No matter how senseless or foolish my action seemed to be, I relied on the Holy Spirit "to guide me into all truth, a step at a time." Although I had faith, human nature is always what we have to continue to work on until we can be conformed to His nature. I was sad to leave all behind, as well as being afraid of the unknown. My leaving could not be understood because I was a well-established young lady, having my own car, house helpers and working in the American Embassy where I was loved and respected! I had all the flexibility to travel to different parts of the country and go to and from Kenya! Leaving all that to go to Sweden, not even America really did not make sense!.

As the day of departure approached, my boss and others in the office tried to convince me to go to America where all was set, instead of going to where I did not know anyone! That made sense but I told them NO. Obeying God does not mean you avoid inconveniences or risks. My boss was ready to contact the Department of State (the Africa Section), but I refused. Then everyone thought I was insane or that I had a hidden agenda in going to Sweden. In this faith journey, I have come to realize, no matter what you say, especially in the context of spiritual experiences, people can doubt you or dismiss you — there is nothing you can do. Yes, they can doubt what you say but they can never take away your experiences nor can they nullify God's grace upon your life.

Secondly, you have to know that depending on the leading of the Holy Spirit to go on missions or to do something that has never been done before, does not mean it will be smooth sailing. Psalms 34:17 says, *"A righteous man may have many troubles, but the Lord delivers him from them*

---

all*. This is the beauty of kingdom life; you have to depend on the Holy Spirit totally. God did not protect Daniel from being misunderstood and wrongly accused when he was thrown in the lion's den. The hungry lions could not eat Daniel because God shut the lions' mouths (Daniel 6:22). I like to also think that when the lions rushed to try to kill Daniel, when he fell in their den, they saw a different Lion, "the Lion of the tribe of Judah in Daniel." The other lions bowed their heads to Daniel and slowly moved backwards.

Yes, there are many hindrances if you try to be led by the Holy Spirit in fulfilling the Great Commission. You will be misunderstood, but don't give up. God did not stop the early Church apostles from being put in prison. Instead, he opened the prison doors! (Acts 5:18.) God did not prevent those who beat Peter, bound his hands and feet, and then threw him in prison. But the chains fell off! No matter who tries to stop God's destiny in your life – as long as you obey God and depend on the leading of the Holy Spirit according to His Word, you will always be victorious. When Church leaders understand and teach that Christology is related to pneumatology, the Church will be equipped to be a mission-oriented entity, and more members will be involved in fulfilling the Great Commission until every sphere of society is touched by the power of God.

Although my church was involved in evangelism and church planting, there was no teaching about members being missionaries to other cultures. To accept going to a foreign land meant having no one to look up to for support or to call when I faced challenges. The only thing was to encourage myself that whatever I might face, God was taking me through training. Willingly, I left Tanzania. The minute I arrived at Arlanda airport in Stockholm, Sweden, I realized I was in a country where they did not speak English but SWEDISH! Immediately I complained to God, "how could you do that?"

CHAPTER FOUR
LORD! THEY DON'T SPEAK ENGLISH?

In order to get more details of my Journey to Sweden, please get my book; <u>Blind Faith: God's Amazing Miracles.</u> In this chapter I will deal with how I managed to overcome all kinds of obstacles in obedience to His leading, especially when people who spoke English came to ask me questions as to why I was in Sweden. When I answered them, "God sent me here as His missionary", they looked at me with puzzled looks and then asked, "what organization has sent you?" Then when I said, "it is not an organization or any church that sent me but God", it was like I had spoken a curse. They did not want to hear it. I remember one man rolled his eyes (that was the first time I saw a man roll his eyes!), and shook his head as if to say, 'young lady – you are crazy!' Laughing out loud he said, "then why did God not teach you how to speak Swedish?" Indeed, why didn't He? I had no answer for him!

On the first Sunday I went to a Church in Bollnas, 500 miles North of Stockholm. No one greeted me or said any words to me. They looked at me and moved away to talk with each other. I am not sure what they were talking, but I thought their conversation was about me. I then kept wondering why God brought me there. I stood waiting for Ruth - an old lady who was sent by God to pick me up from the airport. As I was standing there alone, I was like an East African wooden carving! I was looking but not seeing much because I was busy having my own talk in my mind and blaming God, "How can I witness or talk to anyone if they do not speak any English? I must have made a mistake and I am ready to go home." The reality was psychological unpreparedness! I did not prepare my mind to hear another language spoken because I was conditioned to think that all Europe spoke English- even if they had different nations like Italy, Germany, France, etc. they still spoke English! That was totally not true. Each country had their own language and English was not in their vocabulary.

As a reader you might think I was strange to think that way. Just give me the benefit of the doubt. It was in the 1970s and I was an inexperienced young girl without TV or internet! In this advanced age of technology, there are still people who think Africa is a country! Just ask around- there are still many ignorant people out there. I felt better that I was not alone and it was before internet! Today, many still don't know that there are over 57 countries in Africa and each country has many different languages. For example, in Tanzania alone we have 120 different languages and several dialects. That is why the mission strategy in the 21st century is to use nationals to reach people with their own languages in order to fulfill the Great Commission. The harvest that is plenteous is not in a far country somewhere, but in your neighborhood, in your workplace and even in your churches where there are people who need to be discipled. We have to change or improve some of the strategies in order to attract millennials to advance His Kingdom.

After being among unfriendly Christians that Sunday, I made up my mind to return home. There was no indication that God had meant for me to be there- maybe I did not hear Him properly and had misunderstood Him. In-my helplessness, God sent a young lady ,who spoke some English, to explain that there was no transportation to take me back to Stockholm to the airport which was 500 miles away! I had to wait until Saturday when someone could take me there. God had a different plan and sent someone to take me to Vestros. Then after being there for three days, instead of going to the airport to depart for Tanzania, God vividly spoke to me to go to Orsa, a small town that had a Bible school called Betel Insititutet founded by Ebbe and Ruth Bollin.

When Mr. Bollin heard how I thought I had made a mistake to be a missionary in Sweden, and I was en route back home when God stepped in to send me to Orsa, he laughed and touched my shoulder! Then he said, "You did not miss God because He had shown me a vision of God's *Missionary Girl.* Here you are Nicku, welcome to Sweden". Mr. Ebbe Bollin was big in stature. As he spoke with me, I could sense God's spirit. He told me I was there to be part of his team to help with the students to evangelize Sweden while I would also be learning the Swedish language. He added, "there are some students who understand English, they will help to translate what is happening and you can go with them anywhere to preach. We need that African fire in Sweden" For the first time after eight days of arriving in Sweden, I felt peace and could no longer argue with God. I accepted remaining in Sweden, knowing after the three months stay, I would return home. While there, I was teaching formally and informally all the time. Students were eager to hear my testimonies and life in Africa. Mr. Bollin and the entire Betel Insititutet became my base and family.

God transformed students and many received miracles in their lives while some became my best friends. After a while, I started going with a team to different places to minister. God honored every meeting with miracles and signs. They could not believe God sent me there- it was not something they were used to hearing. In fact, I was getting tired of explaining. Most had never experienced or heard that God still speaks, because many churches were dead spiritually Although God was using me, my mind was to return home. Mr. Bollin wanted me to stay but I told him I had no visa. I had no interest to extend it because it was a long process. A few weeks before the free three months stay expired, I started booking my flight to go home. One afternoon Sister Maillis Ostimo, who was like a school administrator, told me they received a six-month visa extension for my stay in Sweden. When I heard that, I was so upset. I did not tell them to extend it, nor did I desire to stay there. I was homesick and too tired to struggle to try to understand the language or any conversation. Yes, they were very nice people but my feeling that maybe I missed God continued to linger in mind in spite of the vision given to Mr. Bolling. When they sensed I did not want to accept their visa extension, Mr. Bollin promised to take me to Stockholm to attend an International conference so I could be with English speaking people. That night I heard within me a voice say, "you still have work to do here, don't leave."

The following morning, we travelled to a revival meeting in the small town of Malung. Many people came because they wanted to see what an African missionary looked like. Some thought I would have a tail or twelve fingers – they had all kinds of stereotype imaginations. As I ministered through the interpreter from the school, God performed miracles of salvation and healings. One man was deaf and was healed instantaneously, and a woman's leg grew in front of everyone. The following day a woman testified that her ulcers were healed. News continued to spread, and by the third night, God had visited that town. It was when they saw what God was doing, that they started confessing what they thought about an African missionary. They had never seen an African. Some of the things they said were so crazy, it revealed their ignorance. Some were annoying but it did not bother me, it was part of

God's plan to educate me on how to deal with different people and their cultures.

Time came for the President of Betel Institutet, the Administrator Maillis Ostimo and six other students to leave Orsa for Stockholm to attend the international conference held in Citykyrkan, the largest Pentecostal Church in Stockholm. I was very excited because Yongi Choo, the famous speaker from South Korea who then had the largest church in the world, Robert Schuller of the Crystal Cathedral California, a California rancher Demos Shakarian who started the largest network in the world of Christian businessmen called The Full Gospel Business Men's Fellowship International and many other speakers from the USA, Canada, Israel and England were speakers. As we arrived, the students and teachers went to stay in different locations and I stayed with the President and the Administrator in a very nice apartment in an upper-class neighborhood near the city.

When we went to the conference, I was taken to sit on the platform with all the dignitaries and speakers and I was introduced as God's African missionary in Sweden. I felt blessed to represent God and my people of the continent with dignity. I felt God's goodness and mercy following me to continue to practice what James 4:10 says, *"Humble yourselves before the Lord, and he will lift you up."* The services were uplifting. I felt as if I was in heaven. To hear and sing in English made me so happy. During the break, I told my friend to go with me on the street to witness. Remember, since I had arrived, I was in small towns were people did not speak English so I could not go out to witness. Being in the capital, an international city, I targeted winning foreigners, especially Africans because I was hearing bad testimonies that reflected how they represented us. I was on fire to tell them about Jesus and it seemed God prepared them for us. We were able to win several people and some followed us to the meeting. I told Sister Maillis that on Thursday I was going to invite diplomats starting with the Tanzanian Embassy.

God is truly amazing! In spite of all my complaining and arguing with Him that I did not want to be there, He still chose to use me. In spite of not spending much time in biblical prayers, like I used to do at home, God still chose to be patient with me. Although I had more time to study and pray, my prayers were mixed with more complaining and rebellion of not wanting to be in Sweden. In spite of all my weaknesses, God remained faithful. I realized, God being a good Father, knows

His children will fail or falter. He knows we will struggle and face different challenges no matter how well we were nurtured or lacked it. He knows all our shortcomings, yet God does not dilute His love towards us, or change His mind about us! Above all, He does not change the good plans He has for us, otherwise He could have done that with me. It seemed that since I arrived in Sweden, I was not praising Him. I even stopped saying, "your will be done Lord" and instead said, "Lord, I don't want to be here!"

The day came when we went to visit the Tanzanian Embassy. When I introduced myself and told them how God brought me to be a missionary/evangelist and I was in Stockholm attending a conference, they started laughing because they had never heard anything like that, and thought I was joking. I continued to invite them and said, "I think if you come to the evening revivals, the Embassy will be blessed." They once again all laughed so hard with unbelief. One officer said, "How can a Tanzanian girl be a missionary here? You must be out of your mind!!" Each said sarcastic words that did not matter at all. The political officer said, "wait I will tell the Ambassador to meet you." He came back and took me to his office while my friend remained to talk with the other officers.

The Ambassador was very nice but he also did not believe. He invited us to stay and have lunch with him and other officers. I agreed because it was an opportune time to witness to them.

There were seven people at the dining table including the two of us. The first thing the ambassador said was, "officers, have you met our missionary?" They all laughed and said in Swahili, "HAIWEZEKANI! Wala haonekani hivyo" meaning, IMPOSSIBLE -she does not even look like it. He then continued to ask, "now young lady, I know we have a good relationship with this country. Tanzanians can come to Sweden and stay three months without any visa. Many ladies come either to look for easy money for shopping, some try to study or they come for holidays, but no one has ever come as a missionary. It does not happen and it does not make sense!" Then several officers gave their sarcastic comments, and then the Ambassador continued, "You said you left a good job with the American Embassy. Are they the ones who sent you here?" They all seemed to stop chewing and looked at me while I laughed and said, "please come with us to the conference and meet my host and other students from Orsa to know that indeed God sent me to be His witness in Sweden and the entire Scandinavia!

The diplomatic conversation on the lunch table was more in Swahili with a few English statements for the benefit of my friend. Although they all tried so much to convince me that I had made the worst mistake of my life, I did not mind. In fact, we had a great time. Before we left, the Ambassador and the entire diplomatic team were very hospitable, and one local staff agreed to come with us to the conference. He went to sit with my friend and I promised to see him after the meeting. However, when the conference was over, I could not find him because it took a while for me to leave the platform. Though I did not introduce him to anyone, I was glad he came and saw that what I was telling them was not a pretense, but a lifestyle that I have chosen of putting God above any other thing in my life. Nevertheless, I am aware people are entitled to whatever opinion they choose, and that did not and does not worry me.

After we returned to Orsa, I continued to count the months left before I would return to my beautiful Tanzania. But before I returned, I wanted to buy offering plates, organs and guitars for my home churches. Even if I could not get any other things, I had to get the unique offering boxes that I loved. Every church I ministered in had beautiful square silver offering bowls that had two handles and a cross on each side. Every time I saw them, I said, "God, make sure I buy those to take to Dar es Salaam AG Churches and Masebe Lutheran Mission Church in Mwakaleli." I did not have a desire to get anything except things to beautify the place of worship and to enhance God's work. Although I had the desire to buy those things, I had no idea how I would get the money or a job, except to keep thanking God to make sure He found a way for me to get those things before I returned. The Bible in Matthew 6:7-8 says,

> "And when you pray, do not keep on babbling like pagans, for they think they will be heard because of their many words. *8 Do not be like them, for your Father knows what you need before you ask him."* Amen!

Two months before the end of my visa, I saw an advertisement that said the Tanzanian Embassy was interviewing for a position in the tourist section. They were looking for someone who spoke three languages: English, Swedish and French. When I saw it, I was filled with joy. I called my friend Doris and showed her what they had advertised! She saw how excited I was, but then she said, "Kara Nicku (Dear Nicku) they need someone who speaks French and Swedish, and you don't know any of them!" I replied, "That is ok. God has given me this job and I will send them a note requesting the application form." I continued to praise God as if I already got the job. I started visualizing my move to Stockholm and staying in Maillis's house, the same area we stayed during the conference.

As I continued to daydream in faith, I kept telling my friend Doris my plans. She would look at me with a questioning look! But at the same time, she remembered several miracles and testimonies she had experienced since we met! She would cautiously say, "Yes, I know God answers prayer, but this is Sweden! Things are different and you are dealing with diplomats! It does not work that way here" I tried to explain, that when you are walking by faith and living in God's Kingdom on planet earth, you do not depend on what works or not. You depend on the Holy Spirit to lead you and as you "kingdom talk" , God will open doors. I told her, "just agree to go with me back to Stockholm when I am called for the interview!" She quickly said, 'ok, I will definitely come with you." She answered willingly because she was convinced it was impossible for me to be called for an interview. Yet I was convinced I got the job even before the interview. I thought and spoke those things that were not as though they were!

A few days later, the embassy responded and gave me a date for the interview. I asked Sister Maillis if we could stay in her classy apartment, but she refused. I did not mind so much because it was just a one day stay. Instead we stayed with my friend Doris's brother. On the day of the interview at the Embassy, I met eight beautiful, sophisticated ladies, who seemed more experienced and were showing off by talking in French and Swedish. I almost wanted to leave because I felt inadequate. But I encouraged myself. I reminded God why I needed the job. It was so I could buy offering plates and other things for churches! I kept telling Him, "I thank you because you told me I have found favor in your sight, so the job is mine!" I continued rehearsing those words over and over without worrying about the interview questions. I think I was the fifth person to be interviewed. When I entered the interview room, there were three Swedish men and one Tanzanian present. To this day, I do not remember what I said in that interview.

Before I left, I was told that they would decide and let me know in two days' time if I qualified or not. I thanked them and we left the Embassy. As soon as we left the office, I hugged Doris and said, "thank you for coming with me; I got the job." She was puzzled because I told her we would know in two days, but then just a few minutes after the interview, I told her something else. She was confused and she kept on looking at me as I continued to daydream of living at Sveavagen 130TR2, and how I would be able to evangelize and take new converts to Citykyrkan. That was the conversation with my friend, but even with my own small talk, it was filled with thanksgiving for the opportunity to work in Stockholm, to witness in the streets and win people with the love of Christ!

Although I had no assurance of getting the job, nor did I know where I would live, I just looked back at God's dealing with His missionary girl!! I knew God would honor my request because He promised that He will hear me if I obey HIM. Sister Maillis told me several times that no one was allowed to live in that apartment. But I took myself as seriously as God sees me! I knew He took me there, so He was the one to provide for all I needed. I wanted to work for one month, get some money to buy church gifts, then fly back home. I had faith that God would give me favor! Indeed, after two days I received a call that I got the job and that I should report to the embassy in five days. When I told Maillis she said,

"good, you got the job, but you will not stay in the apartment."
I asked Mr. Bollin if he would allow me to live there, but
everyone said it was impossible. My friend had several other
suggestions, but my spirit had only one desire- Sveavagen 130.
I kept on thanking God for what seemed impossible – to give
me the apartment

One scripture I recommend that we need to live by is
Romans 4:16-21

"16 *Therefore, the promise comes by faith, so that it may
be by grace and may be guaranteed to all Abraham's
offspring—not only to those who are of the law but also
to those who have the faith of Abraham. He is the father
of us all. 17 As it is written: "I have made you a father of
many nations."[a] He is our father in the sight of God, in
whom he believed—the God who gives life to the dead
and calls into being things that were not. 18 Against all
hope, Abraham in hope believed and so became the father
of many nations, just as it had been said to him, "So shall
your offspring be."[b] 19 Without weakening in his faith, he
faced the fact that his body was as good as dead—since he
was about a hundred years old—and that Sarah's womb
was also dead. 20 **Yet he did not waver through unbelief***

regarding the promise of God but was strengthened in his faith and gave glory to God, [21] being fully persuaded that God had power to do what he had promised." (Romans 4:16-21)

From that time onwards, every time I saw Maillis, I said to her, "thank God for Sveavagen 130." She would be so upset but it did not matter. I just kept thanking God for her beautiful apartment. My reasoning for holding on to it was simple. It was the first apartment I lived in, and to me, it was not a coincidence, but God's way of meeting all my future needs! That is why I kept on thanking her for the apartment. Everybody thought I was crazy, but I was living and acting upon scripture. One day before I had to leave Betel Institutet for good, Sister Maillis came and handed me the key to the apartment saying, "Nicku, I could not sleep because God told me to give you the key for the apartment. Tomorrow we will take you to Stockholm instead of going by train." Wow! No one could believe what God had done. Before we left, everyone wanted me to pray for them and lay my hands on them for impartation. The power of God fell and I left knowing my mission in Orsa was accomplished.

CHAPTER FIVE

LUNCH IS HARVEST TIME IN STOCKHOLM

As I have continued to participate in this university of life, I have discovered some other reasons why many did not believe God could have sent me as a missionary. Many believers do not understand the plan, purpose and God's will for creating them! Some live, trying hard to know God's will for their lives. Moreover, many people do not understand why the Church exists. In those days, many people used to think that mission work was for the New Testament Apostles or for organizations assigned to do missions, instead of it being an individual mandate. Biblical missions show that God speaks to individuals. We have a good example of how He called Abraham to go to a foreign country to be a father of many nations (Genesis 12:1-3). He also called Moses to go before the King of Egypt to intercede for the release of the Israelites from slavery (Exodus 3:6-10).

In the household of Jacob, God also used a family feud and sibling rivalry, which turned into a murder plot, against Joseph in order to advance His mission. In that crisis, Joseph's attitude to continue to trust God was because he understood that God's plan for his life was to tell others about God's love for them. God's plan for you is good, even in bad situations. Because Joseph had a good heart and attitude towards those who sold him, he found favor even in a foreign land! When you read the life story of Joseph, you will see providential circumstances throughout his life. God protected and used Joseph to be His witness until he won the heart of the king to know that God was with Joseph (Genesis 41:39-43). That is why the New Testaments says, *"By their fruits, you shall know them!"* Not seasonal fruits but a consistent lifestyle – not just in church but everywhere (Matthew 7:16-21). As children of God, we must live knowing that we are carriers of God's will which must be fulfilled on earth. You do not have to be in the Five-Fold Ministries. As long as you are a Christian, God's plan for you is to live and share the Agape love of Jesus Christ anywhere you are! Even if people mistreat you, talk about you or do not appreciate your giftings, do not worry- just focus on pleasing God like Joseph did. Know that you are created and called to be a carrier of Good News!

I started working as a temporary local employee at the Tanzanian Embassy in Stockholm. Many thought my fire for God would be quenched by the many things that attract others, especially young people. Some were anticipating seeing me backslide or start compromising my kingdom lifestyle. I thank God for His grace upon my life, as well as my own choice and determination to be in consistent communication with the Holy Spirit so that His grace will continue to flow without any blockage within my life. In I Corinthians 15:10 Paul said:

> "But by the grace of God I am what I am, and his grace toward me was not in vain. On the contrary, **I worked harder than any of them,** though it was not I, but the grace of God that is with me".

Throughout the scriptures, individuals took their mission assignment seriously because they understood God was the center of the mission, and they had a personal encounter with Him. When you are fully persuaded that you were born, and you are alive because you have a mission to advance His kingdom anywhere and in any profession, every day will be approached with anticipation to tell someone about God's love for them. In that context, I saw every person who came to the embassy as a candidate to hear the Good News, not being "preachy" all the time, but applying Godly wisdom on how to deliver the message that would attract them to hear more. Outside, I used simple strategies to witness and also changed the slogan we used in Nairobi as Young Christian Ambassadors Fellowship with Apostle Joe Kayo which said, "Each One Reach One". In order to make sense and to motivate me to fit my situation, I changed the slogan to being "Each Lunchtime Reach One"

Since the streets of Stockholm were filled with people from around the world, I was determined to use my lunch hour to witness, and many were won for Christ. I kept taking them to my local church and sometimes I gave them the contact information of the church leadership. After a while, I suggested to my senior Pastor Stanly Skorbeg that we have a Sunday afternoon English service to accommodate the new converts and the English-speaking diplomats. He was so excited, and the English service church started to grow. It was awesome and fulfilling to see God using simple faith to change lives. Often, I feel sorry for those who are blinded to only require complicated methods instead of contextualizing strategies where many souls would be reached. In spite of what God was doing, my flesh continued to be homesick because I was living with a feeling of, "mission accomplished!"

After working there for two months instead of one month as planned, I started preparing for my journey back home. I got the money to buy gifts for several churches. I felt the work God sent me to do was over. The faith of many Christians was enhanced, and some churches experienced revival. Above all, many lives had been changed, especially when I thought of the souls saved every lunchtime. I knew it was God leading me to speak to someone who was ready to accept Christ. In the office my testimony was intact! I was a good employee who did not compromise, yet befriended everyone and loved even those who tried to undermine me. All this was possible because of His grace and my personal choice of living in the reality of the Word of God. It is a personal choice and determination to be Christ like, not in church only but everywhere. Read Colossians 1:9-12.

"For this reason, since the day we heard about you, we have not stopped praying for you. We continually ask God

to fill you with the knowledge of his will through all the wisdom and understanding that the Spirit gives, **so that you may live a life worthy of the Lord and please him in every way: bearing fruit in every good work,** *growing in the knowledge of God, being strengthened with all power according to his glorious might so that you may have great endurance and patience, and giving joyful thanks to the Father, who has qualified you [b] to share in the inheritance of his holy people in the kingdom of light"*.

The Word admonishes us to live a life worthy of the Lord, pleasing Him in every way. I obeyed when He told me to leave my country without any specifications of anything. It is up to us to be in tune with what He requires us to do. One simple fact is **God is real and still speaks.** Every day He desires His children to be Salt and Light, anywhere they are! Unfortunately, most of us have unknowingly put the kingdom lifestyle on the back burner. God's agenda for our lives to serve Him, is covered by personal ambitions and traditions. People are too busy chasing after material things instead of putting God first. When this is done everything promised follows. There must be a paradigm shift in order for the Church to return to fulfilling the Great Commission as well as for individuals to refuse to cover themselves with a façade of religiosity, or even Christianity, that does not fulfill God's will, plan and purpose for one's life.

My employer at the Embassy did not want me to leave, instead they wanted to change my status to work full time. My Church did not want me to leave because I enhanced the congregation, and there was still much to be done with the English-speaking Church. Within me, I did not want to hear anyone telling me not to go home! My life in Tanzania was fulfilling, and I was surrounded by family and friends. My parents raised us well and we enjoyed being so many in our home, singing and laughing. There were no boring moments around the Mwakasege's family. To be away for a long time was unbearable. I continued packing and telling friends in different countries that soon I would be leaving Stockholm and the entire Scandinavian region to return to friendly Africa.

Four days before I paid for my ticket, a telephone rang in the middle of the night and when I picked up the phone a voice said in Swedish, "Nicku, spring inte bort Herren, sanna i Sverige" meaning, "Nicku, don't run from the Lord- stay in Sweden!" I tried to ask who it was, but he did not answer and hung up the phone. As I laid there trying to figure out what that call meant, I felt a strange chill going down my spine. I pulled the cover over my head, but it did not help. I started feeling very cold, and then I knew God was speaking! Angrily, I got up as if to say, "God let's talk! What more do you want me to do? I have been in Sweden for ten months; I have done all you wanted me to do!! I want to go back to the good life among my people and go back to my job!" As I knelt there fussing with Him, I felt a strong breeze as if the window was open. I stood up and walked to the window to check if it was open, but it was locked. As I went back to the bedroom, I vividly heard echoes all around me, "Don't run away from God, stay in Sweden"

I screamed out loud, "THIS IS NOT FAIR!" Swedish people are very nice but their culture is very cold and unsocial. Also, their winters are very long. "I cannot stay here, although they have beautiful summers. I want to go home!", I said to myself. I behaved like a child. Although obeying God is one of my life's desires, that does not come so easy, as I am sure you noticed as you read my story. That night I had to face the reality that God wanted me to stay, nevertheless, I had to bargain with Him and said, 'please, allow me to go home, but

I promise to return after one month." I did not want to wait for His response. The next day I went to the Administrator and told him that I would take the Ambassador's offer to work full time but that I needed to go home to give the churches the gifts I had bought for them. He spoke to the Ambassador and they allowed me to travel home and stay three weeks instead of a month. The City Church leadership team was excited to hear that I would return. I left and took the best offering silver vessels for several churches, some of which are still being used today. Those who were skeptical of my call, when they saw me back still on fire, heard the testimonies and looked at some of the pictures, they then believed God had indeed sent me as His Missionary Girl in Northern Europe.

I had told the owner of the apartment in Sweden that I needed to use it for only one month, but then I extended it to two months. The night God told me I should not leave Sweden; another bargaining chip was about the apartment. I would agree to stay if He would perform a miracle for me to continue to live at Sveavagen 130. Indeed, when I called Orsa and told Mailis Ostimo that I was going to Tanzania for three weeks and would return to continue the mission work while I worked at the Embassy, she willingly said, "Yes, Ebbe Bollin

---

told me a few days back that God appeared to him and told him about you." When I asked her what God said, she refused to say but simply told me, "when you go home, you will return to your house." Then she added, "Nicku we thank you for coming to Sweden to revive our faith. Leave your things there; no one will come to the apartment until you return." I am sure by now you realize how His grace is upon my life! This kingdom lifestyle is available for every child and it can be yours as well. If you are serious about obeying God, He will be serious with you. His plans for you and your future is good and He knows how to direct you to fulfill it. When Maillis told me that I could continue living in her apartment, it reminded me of Deuteronomy 6: 11, 13-14;17-18:

> "....Houses filled with all kinds of good things you did not provide, wells you did not dig, and vineyards and olive groves you did not plant—then when you eat and are satisfied, [12] be careful that you do not forget the LORD,.......[13] Fear the LORD your God, serve him only and take your oaths in his name. ...Be sure to keep the commands of the LORD your God and the stipulations and decrees he has given you. [18] **Do what is right and good in the LORD's sight, so that it may go**

well with you and *you may go in and take over the good land the LORD promised on oath ....,"*

When I returned to Sweden the second time, I had to look for a language school to learn Swedish, in order to witness better. I was excited about attending the evening language classes because it was a mission field of its own. I saw each person as a good candidate to be won for Christ, and that is what drove me to be friendly, hospitable and approachable. Whatever I do in life is in the context of sharing and showing God's love with others. I recall one Muslim man, named Shaban, who became my good friend because of his devotion to Mohamed and the Quran, and my devotion to Jesus and the Bible. He felt we had something in common without knowing that my friendship had a hidden agenda to win him! When he saw me leading others to Christ, he would ridicule me in the presence of the new converts. He was among the Muslim leaders who came to establish Islam in Stockholm and saw me as a good candidate to become a Muslim for his team.

He targeted me to convert me, but since he could not make me love my Jesus any less, he talked about a book he wanted me to read to "realize" that Jesus was not the son of God. When he handed me the book called, "The Gospel

According to Barnabas," he said, "this book is one of the few copies remaining in the Library of Congress. It is in my possession because the Imam gave it to me to read and use while I am here. Read it and return it to me. I know you will stop telling others to follow Jesus." I laughed and politely said, "thank you, but my love for Him is deeper than being swayed by a book." I went home and started reading it. The introduction could have made me stop; it was talking blasphemous things – but that made me read it all the way through so that I would be able to respond to my Muslim friend intelligently. The book was one of the apocrypha which the first-century followers of Judaism wrote to discredit Jesus.

When I returned the book, he was shocked to hear me say, "thank you for making me fall more in love with Jesus." That threw him off! He did not expect to hear that! The many times that I tried to witness to Him using the scripture, he would tell me about the Quran. It seemed that I was failing to convince Shaban about Jesus, yet I could not give up. When I was getting discouraged, I asked God to show me how to witness to Shaban. One Friday evening, I felt I should tell him to come to my home for some AfriCafe (African Coffee), so we could discuss more about Islam. I really had no plans, but I depended on the Holy Spirit to show me. When he arrived, I still had no idea what to say. When we were having coffee, he shared what his Imam had requested him to do. Because Islam was taking over England, he wanted Sweden to have the best team. As he continued to talk, an idea came to me. I handed him a blank piece of paper and said, "Shaban, let us forget all that we have learned, or have been told by our leaders in our different faiths. Let us forget all that you read in your Quran and what I read in my Bible. Let us forget it all. Tonight, on that blank sheet of paper, write anything you know Mohamed has done for you **personally,** and I will write what Jesus has done for me."

He looked at me thinking I was joking, but I was not. We started writing. I remember my first word was, *"Jesus talked with me this morning. He fills my heart with joy. He has forgiven all of my sins. He has given me an identity that is above culture. He is my best friend. He protects, provides and so on and so on!* I turned the page over and kept on writing, while he was struggling to write three words on the page. I saw that it was hard for him, so I encouraged him to stop. I gave him my paper and told him to read it. When he read what

I had written, he broke down crying. While he was reading, I was talking to the Holy Spirit to bring conviction in his heart. As he set there sobbing, I started praying aloud with all kinds of prayers. I went and laid my hand on him and asked him to repeat the sinner's prayer as led by the Holy Spirit. That evening he received Jesus as his Lord and Savior. Shaban has not been the same since that day. He started winning others for Christ. Can you imagine that it was not preaching or quoting scriptures that changed Shaban, but it was a personal lifestyle that convinced him that he needed Jesus Christ.

When redeemed people become agents of God's mission and kingdom agenda, they use different methods according to the setting in order to win others to Christ. They use their vocations or jobs, whether civil, or political, secular or religious. Anything they do or anywhere they are, they know they are God's representatives called to spread His amazing love. Shaban got saved unconventionally without my planning or strategizing on ways to do it. Because God saw the intentions of my heart, the Holy Spirit gave me the strategy right on time. My doing something about witnessing to him brought the unconventional method that transformed his life and saved many who could have become Muslims.

I remember, in the streets, inviting people to come to my house to eat African food on the weekend. In the earlier Chapter I wrote how some Swedish people had never had contact with an African, and that some wanted to check if I had a tail or six fingers on each hand! I used whatever uniqueness they saw as an advantage which created an opportunity to speak with them, starting with what interested them, such as being an African. I had to emphasize that we were created by the same God who created them and that I had received His love to share with others The millennium technology has made the world smaller. We read about and see other cultures all the time, but in the 70s, it was not so. Nevertheless, every difference was a tool to share His love. Every insult or ridicule was part of my learning on how to pray and minister to them better. My constant, profound awareness of God's presence is the source and basis of all that goes on around me, therefore everything, good or bad, I try to interpret with reference to the divine purpose. People are blessed with sincerity even with all your shortcomings. The world is tired of actors in the Body of Christ. They want to see people who are genuine.

Another advantage was using what I brought from Africa, especially "Coffee". People in Sweden love coffee. It was an easy strategy to invite strangers to come to my house to taste African coffee. Sometimes I would write a card to hand out to strangers. The card said nothing about Jesus but about what interested them, "*Kom till mitt hus och testa det basta afrikanska kaffet pa!* meaning, "Come to my house and taste the best African coffee at my address, Sveavagen 130 tr 2." Beloved reader, you might think that was dangerous and foolish, because bad people could come to my house to harm me! Fortunately, I don't think that way. You might think that a long time ago people were not as bad as now! That is not true, bad people are everywhere. Bad people could get the address to come to my home, but I have done same thing here,-given people my contact address as I witness to them.

I honestly believe God knows my intention in taking the risk to invite strangers to my home. He protects me. Besides, before I go, I pray. Before I hand out any flyers or anything to anyone, I pray and ask the Holy Spirit to lead me to give them to those He wants to get connected to the plan of God for their lives through His Missionary Girl!

Because of those random invitations, many people honored them and came. Each time, I served some food and drinks. There was this particular time I did not have much food except half a chicken and a few pancakes we call "Chapati za Maji" in Swahili. That day God multiplied food in my apartment- over thirty people ate, and still many pieces remained. On Sunday I went to tell my pastor, Stanley, how food was multiplying in my house; he sent a few elders and they ate but the food did not multiply. I told them "you didn't have faith like the unbelievers, otherwise the food would continue to multiply." Another time, different strangers came to my apartment. Among the men who came to drink coffee was a government minister. Without me knowing who he was, he kept saying he loved the coffee and he wanted to introduce it to Norway where he came from. I said that if he was serious, I would introduce him to the Tanzanian Embassy and he could talk with them about importing coffee to Norway. I did not know who he was, except that he was a man who liked my Afri-Café. I continued to do my witnessing and the English service continued to grow.

A few months later the Ambassador told me there was a man who had signed a contract to import coffee from

---

Tanzania to Norway, and he insisted that I should be the one to fly to Norway to promote the coffee. I told him, "Sir I have no problem talking about Afri-Café as long as they will also let me talk about Jesus." They checked with Norway and they agreed. The Ambassador, the Commercial Attaché and three local employees left Stockholm for Oslo in Norway. We were met very warmly and I seemed to take much of the spotlight. I did not know the man who drank coffee in my apartment was the Norwegian Deputy Minister of Commerce. The officials signed their documents and returned to Stockholm the following day. Judy and I remained to promote the coffee all over Norway. We flew in a private jet to different cities, went to big department stores, and passed the Arctic Circle to Bado where they enjoy midnight summers. Everywhere, we arrived like celebrities- we first talked about Afri-Café then every five minutes I talked about Jesus and prayed for people. This great opportunity happened because I dared to invite strangers into my home. When we flew down south to Kristiansand after our presentation, one pastor came and invited me to come to their church.

It is the responsibility of every Christian to carry on the Great Commission's mandate. Every kind of mission is an individual call. Also, the Church should be the basic foundation where people learn different ways about the Biblical approach to missions – going into every sphere of influence in any community or society to make people followers of Christ. Unfortunately, this is not the case. Biblical missions are ignored or forgotten. Nevertheless, I believe that with the coming of the COVID-19 pandemic in 2020, government leaders, scientists and experts seem confused! It is during these times that God is giving the Church 20/20 vision to see the threshold of an unprecedented harvest of souls and the ability to unite leaders for the Kingdom agenda. True leaders, who have the mind of Christ, must focus on God's plan for the Church which is to equip and encourage members to fulfill the Great Commission by going into every man's world to share the love of Jesus.

The New Testament shows clearly that Jesus is at the very heart of missions. Because I am a Christian who loves Jesus and have experienced the greatness of His grace, it compels me to share with others and "go" anywhere He sends me. I understand we all cannot travel far, but we all can live out the Good News of the Kingdom. You are saved from the kingdom of darkness and enter into the Kingdom of Light, which means that each one of us has a responsibility to share and show God's love, and to impact cultures to become Godly cultures in our society, in our workplace, in the lives of politicians, in politics, business and in every dimension of society! That is why Jesus taught us to always pray, "your Kingdom come on earth as it is in heaven". God's Kingdom is already here, and it is your responsibility to actualize it, starting where you are, with the faith you have!

Whatever you do, you can depend on the Holy Spirit to guide you to which strategy you should use to share Jesus with others. God is not limited to the "four spiritual laws" of evangelism. He is the Omniscient God (all knowing). He is always ready to guide you with His counsel (Ps. 73:24a) Isaiah 30:21 says *"Whether you turn to the right or to the left, your ears will hear a voice behind you, saying, "This is the way; walk in it."* In addition, once you are determined to tell someone about the Good News, read Luke 12:12 which says, *"for the Holy Spirit will teach you at that time what you should say."* Note: The Holy Spirit will guide you where to go, not just to travel but also which mall to go to, which person to talk with, as well as give you an idea on how to start your conversation with that stranger. It is not using the same methods all the time. Learn to listen to your helper, the Holy Spirit. You read how Mr. Shaban was saved because the Holy Spirit led me to give him a piece of paper. That was not spiritual, yet God used it to save a Muslim leader.

Once I got employment in Stockholm, I saw myself as an Ambassador for Jesus in that office. I made efforts to be friends with everyone, and some nicknamed me "Jesus Friend". I accepted with joy whatever they called me. Being Jesus' friend was a promotion. I started a fellowship with diplomatic housewives . We met once per month and had low key Bible Studies and practical talks of how to be content in life. More women came to this "Ambassadors Wives and Diplomats Fellowship" because of the breakthroughs and miracles that Jesus did among them. Some learned how to build a trust in their husbands even if they did not live up to it. I encouraged them to always focus on the strengths of their spouses, rather than the weaknesses, and by doing so, they would avoid living miserable lives and would have good health.

I recall when I was in Kiruna, Northern Sweden past the Arctic Circle, I was worshiping and thanking God for bringing to reality what I did not understand in college. I was taught that there are some countries whereby nights are long and days are short during winter times, and in summer, nights are short and days are long. Coming from East Africa, it did not make sense. Our nights and days seem to all have twelve hours all the time! But in the Scandinavian countries, it was not so, especially when I went to Kiruna in the summertime. There was no night. The sun shone all the time , twenty-four hours a day. It was hard for me to sleep. At home, we go to sleep when it is dark!! For twenty-four hours there was no darkness in Scandinavian countries. Oh, how God taught me that we could live 24 hours in His light like Jesus-did! These are some very rich experiences that help me to yield myself to His will and purpose. Paul in II Corinthians 10:15 says:

> *"Neither do we go beyond our limits by boasting of work done by others. Our hope is that, as your faith continues to grow, our sphere of activity among you will greatly expand, [16] so that we can preach the gospel in the regions beyond you. For we do not want to boast about work already done in someone else's territory. [17] But, "Let the one who boasts boast in the Lord."[a] [18] For it is not the one who commends himself who is approved, but the one whom the Lord commends."*

CHAPTER SIX
CHURCH: GOD'S GREATEST INSTITUTE

When you study the history of the Church in the first century, and how they influenced society in the midst of persecution, you will understand that today's church is performing far less than her potential. In the New Testament, the Book of Acts reveals the zeal of the disciples to fulfill God's missions. However, when they tried to focus on their own regions, or to localize God's agenda, persecution came to drive them to other nations where they continued to spread the Gospel. The Church lost her divine power and authority (became less dependent on God) around the fifth century when she became an "official religion of nations." It became an organization with her leaders increasing their roles of authority and power. Worshippers were kept ignorant of the Word of God. They were manipulated and intimidated by the Church's authoritative ways, as if they were being guided by the Word of God.

The Bible was chained to the pulpit only. Members were not allowed to read it. Its message was hidden in Latin, the secret language of the elite and the clergy. The leaders of the church existed in their private world – inaccessible and unaccountable. God's grace was being abused by the system of indulgences established by the church to receive money as payment for the removal of sin, or for ecclesiastical purposes. The church became wealthy as they manipulated God's Word and took advantage of the people. In those days, God raised Reformers who challenged the shameful abuse of scripture.

In Germany, a professor of theology and monk pastor in Wittenberg named Luther felt his faith in the Scripture was under attack by the sale of indulgences. He was determined to challenge the system, by relying on the support of Scripture, against the formal authority of the Church which he had absolutely reverenced. He opposed God's grace being sold! In his zeal to defend the Word of God, he nailed his famous Ninety-five Theses on indulgences to the door of the Castle Church at Wittenberg. Luther wrote the Theses in Latin to challenge the learned and church leadership, while shielding the masses from church corruption. The faith he had learned by studying the scriptures taught that no individual can receive innermost cleansing from either the Emperor or the Pope but from God alone through the power of Jesus' death.

Reformation, or transforming society to follow the right doctrine, does not happen immediately, but it takes years of commitment and sacrifice to see change manifested. Even in the lives of some individuals, it takes a long time for their minds to be renewed. Before Luther stood against the abuse of God's grace in the fifth century church, similar steps taken by Wycliff and John Huss had failed. In one week, Luther's Ninety-five Theses spread all over Germany. The monk and professor became the mouthpiece of the nation. It was not his plan or desire to be a reformer but he took action to explain, biblically, that the Christian faith depends on the Gospel alone. The more they attacked Luther, the more his teaching shattered the old system to its foundation. Around the year 1526, the Edict of Worms outlawed Luther and his followers as heretics who protested to the church being owned by State. Thus, the name, Protestant church, came into being. It was a call for the Church to stand on the scriptures as the rule of the Christian faith. Thank God for Luther's bold steps to reveal that revelation so that everyone can experience God's free gift of grace. His action demonstrated what Paul wrote in II Timothy 2:9-10:

> "for which I am suffering even to the point of being chained like a criminal. But God's word is not chained. [10] Therefore I endure everything for the sake of the elect, that they too may obtain the salvation that is in Christ Jesus, with eternal glory."

I included a little background of how one person, Martin Luther began the church reformation in 1517 because the Church lost her mission focus and became focused on business and conquest. Luther suffered because he did not want the church to be a political official organization but a place where Christ is exalted. Throughout history, God has always started with one person who has a burden and passion to help others. Today we need Church leaders who will come to their senses to evaluate the many activities that are overshadowing the true mission of the church. In fact, some so called churches are human religious organizations which are less than the true Church that is built on the foundation of Christ.

Many of today's churches rely on the groupings of church politics instead of the Apostolic type that is guided by Christ as the Head, through the Five-Fold Ministries. They don't motivate their members to grow and mature in the faith in order to serve God, but rather emphasis is laid on the quality or the giftings they have as leaders. No wonder many churches are facing challenges to articulate with greater clarity, how to motivate the dot-com generation or millennials to appreciate the importance of the local Church in fulfilling her God given potential -as they put God first in all their careers.

The Universal Body of Christ has no geographical location, skin color, nationality, culture or language. God's church is different from man-made religion, which is designed to control and energize followers to focus on the founder. In doing so, many are kept out of focus to Godly assignments for their lives and that of the Church. Because of this misconception or abuse, many have given up on Christianity or on being part of any church. Members have been abused and misused. Jeremiah 23:1-2-says, *"Woe to the shepherds who are destroying and scattering the sheep of my pasture!" declares the LORD.* However, when one understands God's plan and program for the Body of Christ, which is to be operated withing a local Church, there will be excitement and fulfilment to see what God has done and is doing through the local Church. I believe that in these end times God is waking up Church leaders to teach and encourage members to be like leaven - influencing their environment until it is transformed to reflect God's Kingdom

Paul's Pentecostal ecclesiology teaches that the sole purpose of any church order is to "make room" for the Holy Spirit to carry out His work of edifying believers, using the Five-Fold ministers, with as little hindrances as possible. If this revelation is taught and understood, every member of that local body will want to be involved. They will have no time to be absorbed in the petty stuff so many superficial "churchy" folks focus on. Understanding the bigger picture of a local church in the context of the Body of Christ, the less one will be concerned or notice the petty things. The word of God is loaded with teachings to help us live in the Kingdom lifestyle. In II Timothy 2:14-16 says,

> "Keep reminding God's people of these things. Warn them before God against quarreling about words; it is of no value, and only ruins those who listen. 15 Do your best to present yourself to God as one approved, a worker who does not need to be ashamed and who correctly handles the word of truth.

16 Avoid godless chatter, because those who indulge in it will become more and more ungodly."

The Church is not owned by some personalities or denomination but is supposed to be owned by Jesus Christ. In the Gospel of Matthew 16:18, Jesus said, *".... I will build my Church."* When He spoke those words, Jesus used a Greek language. The word for Church is "Ecclesia" which means "to call out from among." In our literal sense or for better understanding, Jesus was saying, "I will build my called out ones" who will be busy fulfilling the Great Commission in every sphere of society they are in. These "called out ones" will put the Kingdom agenda before their own. Indeed, since the Holy Spirit came, Jesus has been calling out and drawing people to Himself. These called-out ones are men, women, boys, girls, teenagers, older folks, and people of different personalities. He placed each one of them in the local Church to be part of His Body

If Jesus is "building" it means that He is "uniting different broken materials by gradual means into a composite whole, or by constructing using different tools." This is what Christ has been doing and continues to do. Unfortunately, many do not understand the purpose of the Church. If they understood that the church is being built to be alive with an eternal dimension, it would revolutionize their frame of reference. By His grace I was called when I was very young and He revealed to me what His church looked like – a church that has broken people who are clay in the hands of the Potter. He sees them being empowered in their giftings as they are being fed and enhanced by the Five-Fold ministers. Some of these members have astonishing desires to share the Gospel with the dying world and are willing to "GO", if they see their congregations' priority change to include different mission programs that are tailor made , or if there is a concern and care for people's spiritual wellbeing as well as their physical and social wellbeing.

As you answer the call to "GO" away from your people for a cross-culture mission, don't leave without understanding the culture of the people like I did. Also, do not to be like some of the old days' missionaries who went into the mission field of "the heathen" with the mindset to change their culture and traditions in order to Christianize them. In fact, in some African countries, missionaries refused to baptize people with African names and if they were dressed in their African outfits they were disqualified. Christianity was brought with the colonial agenda to westernize the heathen. Missionaries who did that failed to understand that "God is the God of culture but is above culture". A responsible missionary will introduce change in accordance with people's way of life. It does not crush or repress anything good or honorable. Yes, being a missionary means to be an agent of culture change, and conversion, as well, means "turning" away from old ways towards "new ways, a basic reorientation in premises and goals, a wholehearted acceptance of a new set of ways affecting the convert as well as a social group in every sphere of activity" (Whiteman, 2002).The change effected must become living parts of the Kingdom culture.

Christianity is supposed to be the very heart and nerve center of every culture. All of society has to feel the powerful transforming influence of the church. This transformation has to be done wisely to avoid the social and cultural disorganization of the people. In I Corinthians 9:22, Paul said, " be all things to all men" He also said, "to the Jew I became a Jew, to the Gentiles, I became a gentile" To reach this understanding one must know how to "empty" oneself in order to be all things to all men. One must remove the colored glasses through which one views all cultures other than his or her own. When he or she looks at others, they will not seem "strange", "odd", definitely inferior and at times disgusting. Colored glasses are removed when one desires to imitate Jesus Christ, the Son of God who emptied Himself and was detached from the heavenly life to become like us. If this is understood, life in general and mission work will be easy. Philippians 2:6-8 says:

"Who, being in very nature[a] God, did not consider equality with God something to be used to his own advantage; [7] rather, he made himself nothing by taking the very nature[b] of a servant, being made in human likeness.[8] And being found in appearance as a man, he humbled himself by becoming obedient to death— even death on a cross!"

The most effective cross-culture missionaries are those with deep appreciation of the diversity of cultures and the important role which cultures play in human behavior. Although there is still very much that anthropologists do not know about culture (the total way of life and mentality of a people), God's Holy Spirit is able to equip you as you "GO". Culture relevancy is an important apostolic principle. It constitutes the basic missionary tool necessary for advancing

God's Kingdom and is indispensable for successful communication anywhere you go. I believe God sent me to Sweden clueless of anything - the people, the language or their culture- so that I could experience how difficult and challenging it was to be among strangers where nobody knows your name and you cannot even understand the language! I also believe that He wanted me to be able to teach and help others to be better prepared for missions. Nevertheless, I am so thankful that my loneliness was nothing in comparison to those who were sent to Communist nations and lost their lives.

Although Communism was a failed experience, it played a major role in the turbulence of the 20th century missions. The threats, horrors and uncertainties of the Iron Curtain, the Berlin Wall that divided Germany into two countries, were realities of life that I was privileged to experience in the short term. Communists attempted to destroy the church and prohibited any form of religion in the USSR. Any missionary caught evangelizing or preaching was imprisoned, tortured or killed. It is believed that over 20 million Christians were martyred under the former Soviet Union Communist rule that controlled all of Eastern Europe, China, Asia, Angola, Mozambique, Cuba and Latin America. Missionary expulsion was normative throughout the communist world. Yet the church survived and, in many places, thrived underground.

When I went to preach in Moscow, Russia, I was divinely protected by a supernatural miracle I wrote in my introduction of this book. Instead of being arrested I was praised by the authorities as they flipped through my Bible thinking it was their Communist manifesto. Indeed, God is faithful.

In 2 Chronicles 16:9 it says: *"For the eyes of the LORD range throughout the earth to strengthen those whose hearts are fully committed to him...."*

Another time, when I was going to communist East Germany, I was always sad when I passed through Checkpoint Charlie best known as the Berlin Wall which was built during the cold war to separate West Berlin and East Berlin. The Berlin Wall also separated families and brought much suffering. One check point was controlled by four nations: Russia, Germany, France and the United States. It was dangerous to go to East Berlin. We had to go as tourists to encourage the underground church, and we also went without Bibles or any Christian literature. Our preaching was delivered in a form of greetings. It was depressing but the people were filled with hope. Before we left, I asked permission to stand on top of the Berlin Wall to proclaim a message from God. With tears for those who were suffering unnecessarily, I declared the wall to fall down. I had heard the testimonies of families who were separated from their parents and I became consumed with seeing them unite in my lifetime and the Berlin Wall falling like the Wall of Jericho. I returned and continued to pray for change. It wasn't until November 1991 that the wall was demolished and communism became a thing of the past. I thank God He has answered many prayers that have transformed nations. Always depend on God to use you to bring solutions instead of being part of those who just talk and criticize. God is watching what you say and how you say it!

One important fact to know before you speak or witness anywhere is how to contextualize the message according to people's good culture. Although I was young when He sent me into European field, He also gave me wisdom and common sense to use to attract people in every walk of life. Indeed, I cannot fathom how I managed to serve with integrity for all those years, except to give Him praise. As quoted herewith, *"Let the one who boasts boast in the Lord. ¹⁸ For it is not the* one who commends himself who is approved, but the one whom the Lord commends."(2 Corinthians 10:17-18) God sent me there, and I saw how He opened different doors in different countries and churches and even being employed in the Embassy. You would think that my desire to return to Tanzania would stop. Well, it did not.

Anywhere I am, my desire is for God to continue to use me to enhance the local body. As a missionary/evangelist, I still had a local body, as I enlarged His universal Body knowing I would return home. One day I was sent to a church where the pastor openly told me I could not use their pulpit and I had only 35 minutes to preach without asking anyone to be saved or be prayed for. As a pastor of a State Church, he openly said he did not believe in those emotional prayers. Politely I said, "Sir, I can preach from the back if you so desire because the power of His Word and the power of the Holy Spirit is boundless, He can touch people whenever He wants." He smiled and said, "no you will speak from the front near the announcement table." I appreciated him, and then I had a heart talk with my Father, "You heard what he told me! He sees an African girl, but You are in me to deliver many people from this religious spirit. Please take over and transform him."

I sat down and was following the Liturgy while thanking God for doing the impossible. As the pastor called me to preach, he introduced me with a sarcastic smile, 'as I told you, this is the African missionary......'

I stood confidently knowing God would show up. I appreciated the opportunity to be there as I greeted the congregation through the interpreter and started my message. I have forgotten what I preached on, except to remember when the interpreter said the wrong thing, through divine revelation I knew and I corrected him. Some people in the congregation understood English. They asked and wondered how precise I was in detecting wrong statements. I told them it was the power of the Holy Spirit enabling me to do the impossible. Even before I finished preaching, one woman came crying at the altar saying, "I want to be saved and filled with the Holy Spirit." I stopped preaching and went to lay my hands on her. As I started praying, others started coming!! What the Pastor did not want to see, is what God did. He took over the service, people were being healed and others spoke in tongues. I went on for almost two hours and the Pastor was dumbfounded because the first woman who interrupted the preaching was his wife. The deaf heard, a man whose leg was short grew and he had to remove the platform shoes in order to walk normally. Some of the church elders were filled with the power from on High. God showed up and showed off His missionary girl! I was not on my own!

There are many churches hindering people from entering into a full communion with Christ because traditions deny the power and the function of the Holy Spirit. Thank God the 21st Church has advanced because of the Pentecostal and Charismatic movements. Christianity is advancing geographically by using innovative approaches to bring global awareness on how to reach the world for Christ. The mission purpose of God's people is inextricably entwined with the nature of the New Testament church. Christian leaders as well as individuals must renew their commitment to the divine purpose. We must rededicate ourselves to the redemptive task and intensify our efforts to fulfill the Great Commission with great compassion in this confused generation.

There are many sacrilegious practices floating in social media that are shocking and causing the name of the Lord to be profaned by unbelievers. Some of these churches have no idea of any church doctrines. (Ecclesiology), such as Soteriology, Christology, Pneumatology etc. May God raise up people who will reform the church to teach correct doctrines and exalt Jesus. These are the last days. God will raise men from obscurity who are filled with the Holy Spirit and courage to stand against any church authority who want to be exalted by their members more than Jesus who died for them. Above all, any church that emphasizes salvation without mission, forget to realize that salvation is the heart of mission. God is a missionary God and salvation is a divine mission act.

CHAPTER SEVEN
OBEYING TO 'GO' IS MUCH FUN!

" For God's gifts and his call are irrevocable. Just as you who were at one time disobedient to God have now received mercy as a result of their disobedience",

(Romans 11:29-30)

I mentioned how every child of God was born with a specific purpose to build part of God's Kingdom on earth. Every profession, every work or job that you do, is because God put you there to be His witness. If you are a born again, spirit filled person, anywhere is a potential field for harvest. You are not your own. You are working to provide for your physical needs and that of your family, but you are on God's royal service. I pray you will realize, apart from the Lord's work, there is no one single involvement more important than fulfilling God's assignment for your life. You do not have to be in the Five-Fold Ministry (Apostles, Prophets, Evangelist, Pastors or Teachers) to be involved with the Great

Commission. God has given you gifts that will shine His light in any of the eight spheres of society (Government, Economy, Education, Culture, Art/Media, Family, Religion and Sports). The scope of God's world program is limitless. He does not require perfect vessels with qualifications, but rather He uses broken vessels who are not qualified, and He qualifies them. As long as you are willing, or you have learned how to hear the Holy Spirit's instruction, you can indeed work in any field that is ripe with souls who need to hear about God's love, hope and forgiveness.

Once you can speak, you can train yourself to be an evangelist, which means a good news carrier. You can speak good words to encourage someone about how special they are because they are loved by the most powerful Creator. You can speak hope, peace, and satisfaction to anyone without preaching. As you practice, you will start being fulfilled. Once your desire is to be light and salt, the Holy Spirit will direct you where to shine, what to say and how to say it in order to engage the person. You read about the many times I won people to Christ by using common sense. Although I always wanted to go home, God was not through with me. In fact, not everything was bad. I could have been content to be in

---

Sweden living a good life in a great location. I had it all! But that is not what I was born to be or to do. My desire is being in God's perfect will and doing what He wants me to do, that does not conflict with the local church but enhances her mission!

Being in Sweden, I could see the hand of God in many personal situations. Yet in the back of my mind it was like I had missed God. No matter how people were being saved, and the English service continued to grow, that did not convince me that I had obeyed Him totally. Maybe my ego did not want to accept that I was in God's perfect will. Besides, I met many wonderful people who became family. I lived in a beautiful apartment in a high-class neighborhood without paying any rent, yet I was not settled in my spirit. These are some of the tricks the enemy uses to hinder us to live in the fullness of Christ's joy. Nevertheless, later in life I understood why God sent me to Sweden instead of coming directly to America.

At Betel Institutet, I met great young friends who are family to this day. One such friend was Doris Ottosson who spoke good English. We connected immediately with others who could understand English. I remember that one early morning when I saw snow for the first time, I thought the rapture had taken place. I looked everywhere; it was so white and beautiful. "Am I in heaven or have I been left behind?" I wondered to myself. I ran to see if the other girls were still around, because I could not imagine being left alone. When they heard how I felt, they laughed and teased me for some days. One weekend they took me to try skiing. I kept falling down like a log!! It was terrible. The only thing I enjoyed was to slide on a sled like a child.

Don't laugh at me for being too local. In Tanzania we have no snow except on Mount Kilimanjaro, the highest mountain in Africa. However, during the cold season, June to July we see some frost in the high elevated area in Mbeya. Seeing falling snow was very new, especially when I saw how gently it fell. It is so lovely, yet so dangerous. I kept on falling even when I stepped out of the building. I did not have much winter clothes except what they gave me. Even when they taught me how to dress and walk, it took a while. Teaching me to ski was disastrous! Each time they gave me a new pair of skies, they would break. It was hard to learn, yet I did not give up. One time we went with my friend who domesticated moose and Elk in Norrbotten. I was so afraid to step out. They laughed at me and forgot I was their evangelist. In another area, the reindeer pulled us on a sleigh as we visited different families. We rode for hours. I had frostbite; it was painful. It was at that time that I refused to go anywhere. I have many memories of learning how to water ski on the island of Gotland where my friend Lena took me to relax. Those were great times spent visiting different countrysides after being tired ministering, especially with my not knowing the language and trying hard to hear what people were saying! That was the reason, all the time, that I wanted to go home!

The most exciting experience was to be nominated as their "Black Saint Lucia", a tradition that is very popular in Scandinavian countries. It is said that Lucia was an Italian young girl who was martyred because of her faith and brought blessings or good luck to people. Every year they hold a special holiday that occurs on December 13th. Before dawn, young women dress up in white with a red sash around their waists, holding candles and singing as they walk around, and surround Saint Lucia who has lighted candles on her head. Can you imagine how crazy that was for me to act as Saint Lucia!! Yet I agreed. When the time came, I was dressed in white with a red belt, and they put a crown of burning candles on my head!

That day many people came to watch and touch the "Black Saint Lucia" It was so much fun. I became their "Saint" instead of being their missionary. Nevertheless, in my heart I kept praying for Jesus to bless them. In Sweden, especially in the Dalana area, they take this tradition very seriously. They even bake special bread called "lussebullar" made from the expensive saffron spice. It is also known as the Festival of Light, because it falls within the advent season that points to the arrival of the Light of Christ.

It gives me joy to share these experiences in order to motivate you. God is no respecter of persons, but of principle. If you follow what He says, it will happen to you and far much more will. Kingdom living is never boring but exciting and filled with miracles. I have said that obeying God is fun. You live in anticipation of hearing Him or being surprised by Him, because He is God. He does whatever He wills to bless and encourage those who seek to see His Kingdom manifested in the lives of other people. There are different great rewards that God surprises me with all the time. My life is filled with miracles in so many ways. I could write so many books about how God has been dealing with His "missionary girl!"

One day God used a friend to buy a first-class ticket for my mission trip from Washington to South Africa on British Airways. You can imagine how I felt. I felt even more of His anointing being manifested than usual. On my way back, something awesome happened when we landed at Heathrow Airport. Normally first-class passengers disembark first. As I left my seat and walked towards where the flight attendants were, there stood two men wearing dark glasses holding a sign that read - Dr. Mordi! I identified myself while I waited to be told why they were looking for me. Without any motion or a salutation, they just said, "follow us". We entered through a secret door, that opens as soon as the bridge is connected, to the plane and entered a car that was waiting beside the plane. I was not sure what was happening or what to think!

Seating in that car, my thoughts were not good, but were thoughts of bewilderment! Was I being arrested? Why did Scotland Yard's secret police come for me? On and on the thoughts continued. The men were quiet and looked very serious. Nonetheless, after I finished thinking, within me I started saying, "I am innocent" . No matter what they will accuse me of, or if they interrogate me "I am innocent". Even if they have found something in my luggage planted by someone, "I am innocent". There were no thoughts of being spiritual, but thoughts of how to defend myself. It is amazing how our mind works – no one had said anything but I was busy preparing my defense. Not once did I think God was blessing His daughter by giving her a royal welcome after a long fruitful mission trip. In fact, that is what happened. I was not being arrested but being treated like a VIP. Instead of walking to the transit lounge, God sent a special envoy to come and drive me there!

I was the first person in our flight to arrive in the first-class VIP lounge at Heathrow Airport in the United Kingdom. The attendant rushed and took my hand luggage while sitting me next to where another person was waiting with a warm towel. As I was drinking my juice, the other passengers (mostly white males) were shocked to see me, and some came and asked me, "how did you come so fast"? I told them that I did not walk like they did. I was picked up in a special car! They left discussing that among themselves! "That must be a woman of great importance". Another one said, "she must be a wife of one of those corrupt politicians who send their wives shopping etc.!" As they walked to be seated, they kept trying to discuss why I was given a ride and not them! I kept on eavesdropping until they were seated where I could not hear their conversation. In my heart I was smiling and praising God.

Romans 11:33-36 says-*33Oh, the depth of the riches of the wisdom and knowledge of God! How unsearchable his judgments, and his paths beyond tracing out! 34 "Who has known the mind of the Lord? Or who has been his counselor?" 35 "Who has ever given to God, that God should repay them?" 36 For from him and through him and for him are all things. To him be the glory forever! Amen.*

After a while the VIP lounge attendant came to show me where I could rest and take a shower if I wanted to. In my years of travelling, I had only travelled once on a one hour first class ticket on East African Airways, but never on British Airways. To be told I could take a shower and rest was an experience I could not refuse! Though I behaved calm, within me I was filled with shock, shouting and having my invisible hallelujah dance! I put on their silk classy robe and looked at the bed! I just smiled as I went to take a shower and sleep on a very comfortable bed! To this day, I am thankful to the family who gave me the first-class ticket to go on a mission field. I returned home talking more about my flight experience

---

than about the crusades and seminars. Obeying God by doing what you do not understand requires faith and courage. Do not worry if you miss it now and then. It is a lifetime journey, and it is a great thing to live knowing you are serving God according to what He has enabled you to do. Welcome to the life of unmovable faith!

CONCLUSION

Today the Holy Spirit does not manifest much of the supernatural because those who believe have eroded and fostered negative attitudes towards Him. They do not allow Him to be actively involved in their personal lives. They don't hunger for the experiential dimension of the Holy Spirit leading them for missions like He did with the early missionaries, as well as He has been doing with me. Also, messages from many pulpits are not supported by Biblical exegesis, nor have references to the scriptures. If you study the Pastoral epistles, Paul did everything not to attain success by fortifying the church to himself or practicing nepotism, but allowed his followers to use their ministerial giftings for the advancement of God's kingdom agenda.

In recent months, there has been a shifting and a shaking. God is purifying the Church to get ready for Jesus' return. In the midst of the incredible complexity of so much bad news of the COVID-19 virus which has perplexed the world, Christians have been forced to turn to God in repentance. God is drawing people to Himself, bringing them out of old habits,

---

dead works, spending too much time building personal ecclesiasticism and returning them to the New Testament Church. Due to COVID-19, there is unity in the Body of Christ across denominational lines, and different races and nations. Many praying Christian leaders have received revelations of the power they have to decree and declare over the ruling authority in any nation, for the Lordship of Jesus Christ to be established. It behooves all of us to rethink how to behave or conduct church services when the new normal starts – after being quarantined for months. I hope members got the revelation that going to Church is to learn to "Serve" not to **be** served!

I pray we will not go back to some of the old ways of neglecting the true purpose of the church. The new normal will be filled with people who rejoice to gather for "church SERVICE" to advance God's Kingdom. As Five-Fold leaders, we must forsake some of our ways to become like Daniel, a person with an excellent spirit, wisdom and tactics. God is ready to use His church to proclaim the initial and central message of Christ – the Kingdom is at hand! At the same time, every individual Christian must be taught to become ablaze with love, zeal and a godly astonishing desire to be guided by the Holy Spirit to share the Gospel in the helpless, confused and mixed-up world! May God help us to be faithful in that which He has assigned us to do, in any vocation. Our assignment is to advance Christ's mission on earth! Allow Christ to shine HIS Light through you! When you do, God will be with you to bless every step you take. Amen!

ABOUT THE AUTHOR

Dr. Nicku Kyungu Mordi is the President and Founder of International Gospel Outreach Ministries and Africa for Jesus Prayer Movement (I GO AFJ Ministries); founder of Unity in Diversity Ministers Council, and Africa Transformation Embassy. Dr, Mordi committed her life to the Lordship of Jesus Christ at just six years old. She is consumed with fulfilling the Great Commission and touching people with the love of Jesus Christ as shown in Matthew. 25:34-40. Her life is filled with supernatural miracles like those of Abraham. The Lord uses her to miraculously multiply food, command monuments to fall, affect decisions of nations, and use handkerchiefs miraculously as in the Bible. Dr. Mordi's daily life is filled with being intimate with God in words and in deeds. Her child like faith in God is unshakable! She is respected because of her humility, focus and passion to help others. She also serves as International envoy of Bethel World Outreach Church in Olney, Maryland.

Dr. Mordi, who is affectionally known as Mama Africa is a well-known speaker, philanthropist and advocate for the unity of the Body of Christ, and an Apostle to the nations. She has travelled and ministers in 50 countries and has been among presidents, kings and spiritual leaders of our time. Each year she hosts strategic conferences among church leaders and government officials in different countries under the theme: Sustainable *Strategies to Transform Communities and Nations.* In 2007 she organized the first ever historic continental campaign to decree the mind of God in nations and inspire Christians to bring development in their communities until God's kingdom is manifested in the lives of the youth and women.

Her leadership qualities began as a young girl in Tanzania. At just 17 years old, she was sent to India to represent the youth of her country. Her zeal for God caused her to help pioneer the then fastest growing deliverance church in Nairobi, Kenya and plant several Assemblies of God churches in Tanzania. She served as the Executive Director for Morris Cerullo's Crusade under the Assemblies of God Superintendent in

Tanzania. She was elected to the Council of Elders for the Trinity College of Ministerial Arts in Aba, Nigeria (now known as TRICOMA). In 1977 she left a really good job with the American Embassy in Dar es Salaam and all her possessions to obey God and become a missionary/evangelist in Sweden, Scandinavia.

For years Dr Mordi hosted the African Ambassadors monthly strategic governmental Bible studies and Unity in Diversity Ministers Fellowship in the Washington Metropolitan Area; Godly Women of Excellency Empowerment Seminars and hosted the AFJ Annual Conference to unite African churches in USA. Once a year she challenges Christians to offer thanksgiving prayers to unite governments and civil servants for the peace of their nations. Dr. Mordi has received several leadership awards. In 1990 she received the Meritorious Achievement Award from the International Affairs Leadership Parliament in California. In 2009 she received a distinct Women's award from the President of the Democratic Republic of the Congo. In 2011 she received a Humanitarian Award from His Majesty the King of the Zululand in South Africa. In 2013 she received a Citizen's Purple Heart Award from the US Municipal Guard Law Enforcement. In 2014 she received an award from Who's Who among Executive & Professional of Impact. In 2016 she received a USDA Women in Public Service Award and in 2018 she received an honorary PhD in Philosophy from the Trinity International Bible University of South Africa and an Impact to Africa Outstanding Award 2020 from Destiny Women International in Liberia and much more.

Dr. Mordi holds several academic degrees: Bachelor of Arts, a Master's Degree in Divinity and a Doctorate degree in Ministry from the Oral Roberts University in Tulsa Oklahoma. She is the author of five books and writes gospel tracts. She is also the founder of the Hope Africa Newspaper. Dr. Mordi is married to Elder George and they have two children and three grandchildren.

Other Inspiring Books By The Author

God's Finger on My Bedroom Wall : Could this be an End-time Strategy?

*Never Forgotten: Advice for All God's Children

Get Ready for Change: A Prophetic Revelation

God's Emancipation: Deliverance Through Christ

Do You Know What Hinders Your Prayers?

*Blind Faith: God's Amazing Miracles

Foundational Children Books

*Next Generation: Do you know who you are?

 *Next Generation: Know Before You Grow!

Soon To Be Released

Unmovable Faith: Do you get in a Home or in a House?

You can contact Dr. Mordi by email at

igoministries@yahoo.com

or through the ministries' websites –

www.igoafricaforjesus.org and www.atembassy.org

References

Whiteman, D. L. (2002). *An Ethnohistorical Study of Social and Religious Change in the Southwest.*

Made in the USA
Coppell, TX
23 December 2020

45336434R00069